VIRGINIA LANDMARKS OF BLACK HISTORY

SITES ON THE VIRGINIA LANDMARKS REGISTER

AND THE NATIONAL REGISTER OF HISTORIC PLACES

Michael Plunkett
Afro-American Sources in Virginia
A Guide to Manuscripts

Sally Belfrage
Freedom Summer

Armstead L. Robinson and Patricia Sullivan, eds.
New Directions in Civil Rights Studies

Leroy Vail and Landeg White
Power and the Praise Poem
Southern African Voices in History

Robert A. Pratt
The Color of Their Skin
Education and Race in Richmond, Virginia, 1954–89

Ira Berlin and Philip D. Morgan, eds.
Cultivation and Culture
Labor and the Shaping of Slave Life in the Americas

Calder Loth, ed.
Virginia Landmarks of Black History
Sites on the Virginia Landmarks Register
    and the National Register of Historic Places

VIRGINIA LANDMARKS OF BLACK HISTORY

SITES ON THE VIRGINIA LANDMARKS REGISTER
AND THE NATIONAL REGISTER OF HISTORIC PLACES

Prepared by the Virginia Department of Historic Resources

Edited by **CALDER LOTH**

UNIVERSITY PRESS OF VIRGINIA

Charlottesville and London

THE UNIVERSITY OF PRESS OF VIRGINIA

Copyright © 1995 by the Rector and Visitors

of the University of Virginia

First published 1995

LIBRARY OF CONGRESS CATALOGING-IN-PUBLICATION ÐATA

Virginia landmarks of Black history : sites on the Virginia landmarks

    register and the National register of historic places / prepared by

    the Virginia Department of Historic Resources ; edited by Calder

    Loth.

        p.   cm. —(Carter G. Woodson Institute series in Black

    studies)

    Includes index.

      ISBN 0-8139-1600-3.   ISBN 0-8139-1601-1 (pbk)

      1. Afro-Americans—Virginia—History.   2. Historic sites—

Virginia.   3. Virginia—History, Local.   I. Loth, Calder, 1943– .

II. Virginia Dept. of Historic Resources.   III. Series.

E185.93.V8V57   1995

975.5'00496073—dc20   94-32817

                                           CIP

Printed in the United States of America

C O N T E N T S

FOREWORD

I T   I S   I N D E E D a pleasure to introduce this catalog of Virginia's African-American landmarks. As the grandson of former slaves and the first elected African-American governor in the history of our country, I am especially delighted by this volume.

The first Americans who were of African descent came to Virginia in August 1619, more than a year before the *Mayflower* landed in New England. Since then, despite every adversity, Virginia African-Americans have made and continue to make enormous contributions to the state and nation. The story of their achievements is not confined to history books but is told in tangible ways through the historic buildings and sites that add so much to Virginia's landscape.

Too many Americans are unaware of that story. The Commonwealth of Virginia is committed to telling it, however, through places we can see and visit. African-Americans built many of the grand mansions so cherished by Virginians; they fought courageously for their country's freedom in the Revolution and for their own in the Civil War; they built churches, schools, and communities to provide themselves with the benefits of freedom; and they played major roles in shaping the life and culture of Virginia and all of the states.

The Commonwealth is committed to identifying and recognizing the tangible history of all Virginians. This volume is but a first step toward that goal. It is an invitation to all Virginians to share our history of achievement, which belongs to all Americans, of whatever descent. It is also a reminder that Virginia's past, great as it is, is not as great as its future.

I hope that all Virginians will find this book to be a source of inspiration and pride.

LAWRENCE DOUGLAS WILDER

SERIES EDITOR'S FOREWORD

I AM HONORED to call the attention of the reading public to the most recent addition to the Carter G. Woodson Institute Series in Black Studies: this timely and evocative guide of Afro-American landmarks in Virginia, prepared by Calder Loth. As I read the text and examined its striking images, I was awed by the sheer enormity of the black experience in the Commonwealth of Virginia. I could not help but note that 1994 commemorated the two most improbable bookends of the Virginian black experience: the 375th anniversary of the first landing of Africans in English America and the conclusion of the term in office of the first elected black governor in the history of the United States. Three hundred seventy-five years means that it can be fairly said that Virginia does indeed encompass this nation's longest continuous experience of Afro-American life and culture. And this volume provides the first official catalog of the historic landmarks associated with that epic encounter.

Virginia's black experience began at Jamestown settlement, in late August 1619, when a Dutch warship landed "twenty and odd" Africans, the first of the more than four hundred thousand who would come involuntarily to the United States during the period up to January 1, 1808, when Congress officially banned the once-booming transatlantic trade in slaves. The young republic prospered during the so-called Virginia Dynasty, a period when four slaveholding presidents from Virginia laid strong foundations for a transcontinental nation. In 1860, on the eve of the Civil War, the state of Virginia held more slaves than any other of the fifteen slaveholding states in the Union. It was at Fort Monroe, Virginia, in May 1861, that Union general Benjamin Butler first proclaimed wartime runaway slaves to be "contrabands of war," a designation which not only conferred freedom on three refugees from a Confederate forced labor camp but also catalyzed the process that led eventually to Lincoln's Emancipation Proclamation of January 1, 1863.

The Virginia General Assembly made history in 1882 when it established Virginia State University as the nation's first publicly funded segregated institution of higher learning. And in 1956 the state also made history when it enacted "massive resistance" laws to frustrate the implementation of the 1954 Supreme Court decision that had declared segregated education to be unconstitutional. It was ironic that L. Douglas Wilder, the descendant of former slaves, handed over the reins of government to his successor while standing in front of a state capitol constructed by slaves. Thus it is that the many ironies, paradoxes, contradictions, and achievements of the Afro-American experience in the Old Dominion find concrete expression in the rich diversity of the preserved built environment of Virginia.

Interspersed with well-known landmarks in this catalog are entries for lesser-known monuments to the black experience in Virginia. The Banneker boundary stone, for example, highlights the intellectual prowess of the eighteenth-century black mathematician whose memory enabled the recovery of L'Enfant's destroyed plans for the national capital. Lott Cary's birth site commemorates the bold achievements of a little-known nineteenth-century crusader for human freedom. The many sites devoted to black religious and educational institutions tell a story of consistently successful efforts by Virginia blacks to overcome the heritages of slavery and segregation. And the Richmond building in which for many decades Maggie Walker conducted benevolent activities for the Independent Order of St. Luke affirms the tenacity of black Virginian struggles for human dignity and economic independence.

Precisely because a guide to black landmarks is so long overdue, this publication must be viewed as a very positive achievement. It is not intended, however, to inaugurate a continuing series of such publications. Rather, it reflects the recognition that previous guides to Virginia landmarks have failed to provide a comprehensive listing of deserving Afro-American historic places. The guide is, therefore, a means to the end of producing a more fully inclusive edition of *The Virginia Landmarks Register.* And indeed, even before its publication, this particular guide has already done wonderful service, since its preparation led to the addition of numerous Afro-American historical sites to the official list of Virginian historic landmarks.

It is my hope that readers of this guide will become active in alerting the Virginia Department of Historic Resources to places significant in Afro-American history that are not currently listed, so that the next edition of *The Virginia Landmarks Register* will provide the fullest possible level of inclusion for Afro-American historical places. The systematic incorporation of landmarks of Afro-American experiences into the official catalog of Virginia historic places will mark a significant breakthrough in the long-standing effort to accord to the black experience its proper emphasis in the grand narrative of the history of Virginia. This is an emphasis that the black experience has long merited.

The reader will notice that varied terms are used here to designate peoples of African descent. Disputes about the proper term designating peoples of African descent have occupied black intellectuals for at least two centuries. During this lengthy period favored terms have included, for example, people of color, African, colored people, Ethiopian, Negro, Afro-American, black, and most recently African-American. The persistent difficulty of devising terminology sensitive to the demands of racial identity (skin color), on the one hand, and of cultural identity (place of origin), on the other, accounts to a quite significant extent, for the lack of settled consensus on this contested issue. In addition, the fact that black people in the United States came from the continent of Africa with its racially mixed population further complicates the symbolic politics of racial-cultural identity. It is for these reasons that the text, often reflects the multiplicity of terminologies that remain the historical record of contested naming practices in black America.

The central theme of this volume is inclusiveness. It seems to me that at this stage in the history of our national culture the common wealth surely lies in the direction of producing a pluralist narrative which accords proportionate emphasis to the diversity of our shared history. It is my fond hope that this volume will contribute to a more fully inclusive commemoration of Virginia's past. Certainly, the estimable effort by the Virginia Department of Historic Resources and by Calder Loth to prepare this marvelous guide measure the vast distance we have trod these 375 years toward a goal unimaginable to the first "twenty and odd" Africans who involuntarily came ashore at Jamestown settlement in August 1619.

ARMSTEAD L. ROBINSON

PREFACE

THE VIRGINIA LANDMARKS REGISTER

T H E Virginia Landmarks Register was established in 1966 with the legislation establishing the Virginia Historic Landmarks Commission, the present successor to which is the Virginia Department of Historic Resources. The legislation charged the department with the task of perpetuating "those structures and areas which have a close and immediate relationship to the values upon which the state and nation were founded." To carry out that task, the legislation directed the department to make a general survey of the state's historic resources and to designate as historic landmarks the buildings, structures, sites, and historic districts that constitute the principal historical, architectural, and archaeological sites of local, state, or national significance. It was agreed that the list of designated historic landmarks would be called the Virginia Landmarks Register and that the entries made to it would be called Virginia Historic Landmarks.

Although the department's staff of historians, architectural historians, archaeologists, and other specialists proposes and processes nominations to the Virginia Landmarks Register, the actual designations are made by the Board of Historic Resources, an independent board whose primary functions are to make additions to the Virginia Landmarks Register and to advise the department on preservation matters. The board is composed of seven private citizens of the Commonwealth, appointed by the governor. For a property to be registered, it must meet established criteria. In meeting the criteria it is essential that the property preserve sufficient historic, architectural, and/or archaeological integrity.

Nominations to the Virginia Landmarks Register may be generated either by the department's staff or by any interested individual. Frequently nominations are proposed by the property owners themselves. Listing on the Virginia Landmarks Register can be a lengthy process. Each proposed designation requires a nomination report containing a detailed description, a statement, of significance, supporting documentation, a map, and photographs. The report may be prepared by the staff, by members of the public, or, most commonly, by professional consultants. Approval by the Board of Historic Resources attests that a property conforms to established criteria and is of significance to the Commonwealth. The board presents the owners or custodians of designated properties with a plaque stating that the property has been registered as a Virginia Historic Landmark. The board will not register a property if its owner formally objects.

Listing on the Virginia Landmarks Register does not restrict an owner's use of his or her property. Architectural controls, such as are imposed through historic district zoning, can be established only by local governing bodies. Registration is primarily an official recognition that a place is an outstanding historic resource and is worthy of preservation. The staff of the Department of Historic Resources is prepared to assist in an advisory capacity with the preservation of any registered landmark.

THE FEDERAL PROGRAM

Virginia's preservation program is closely aligned with a highly structured federal preservation program. The National Historic Preservation Act of 1966 called for the expansion of the National Register of Historic Places to include properties of state and local, as well as national, significance and charged the states with the responsibility of submitting nominations to the National Register. The National Register of Historic Places is maintained by the National Park Service within the Department of the Interior. Regulations governing the National Register require each state to establish a State Review Board to examine and make recommendations upon proposed nominations to the National Register. In Virginia the State Review Board members are appointed by the director of the Department of Historic Resources. The Board of Historic Resources and the State Review Board act in close cooperation so that proposed nominations generally receive the same treatment from both of the boards. As the National Park Service ordinarily accepts the nomination made by the states, the Virginia section of the National Register, for the most part, contains the same entries as the Virginia Landmarks Register.

NATIONAL HISTORIC LANDMARKS

Under the authority of the Historic Sites Act of 1935, the secretary of the interior, upon recommendation by the Advisory Board on National Parks, Historic Sites, Buildings, and Monuments, may declare a property to be a National Historic Landmark. The National Historic Landmark designation signifies that a property is of national significance in addition to being of state or local significance. The owner of such a property is offered a certificate and a bronze plaque stating the designation. In accepting the plaque the owner agrees to preserve those significant historical values for which the property was designated. The Board of Historic Resources may be consulted on properties under consideration for National Historic Landmark status but generally does not play an active role in the program.

Information on having a property listed on the Virginia Landmarks Register and the National Register of Historic Places may be obtained by writing

> The Registrar
> *Virginia Department of Historic Resources*
> *221 Governor Street, Richmond, Virginia 23219-2010*

A CAUTIONARY NOTE

Many properties included in this catalog are privately owned and not open to the public. Some places are open to visitors on a regular basis; others may be visited by special arrangement or on special occasions. Those properties that are maintained as museums have been noted, for the most part, in the catalog entries. The most up-to-date general listing of historic properties open to the public is maintained by the Visitor Information Office, Bell Tower, 101 North Ninth Street, Richmond, VA 23219-2010; telephone: (804) 786-4484. More specific inquiries about the public accessibility to privately owned landmarks should be addressed to the Information Officer, Department of Historic Resources, 221 Governor Street, Richmond, VA 23219-2010; telephone: (804) 786-3143.

ACKNOWLEDGMENTS

The editor wishes to thank the following individuals who kindly assisted with this publication.

Osceola S. Ailor, *Little England Chapel*
Ann Bailey, *Roanoke*
Joe Berryman, *Virginia College and Virginia Seminary*
Harry A. Butowsky, *National Park Service*
Cary Carson, *Colonial Williamsburg Foundation*
Robert A. Carter, *Virginia Department of Historic Resources*
Edward A. Chappell, *Colonial Williamsburg Foundation*
Jean Currie Church, *Howard University*
Michael Cobb, *Hampton Arts Commission*
Molly Converse, *Loudoun County Public Schools*

William Cosby, Sr., *Virginia Randolph Museum*

Elizabeth S. David, *Fairfax County Heritage Resources Branch*

Reverend Alvin Edwards, *Mount Zion Baptist Church, Charlottesville*

Katherine S. Edwards, *Hampton University*

Lucious Edwards, Jr., *Virginia State University*

Libby Fosso, *Thomas Jefferson Memorial Foundation*

Dr. Francis Foster, *Richmond*

Katherine K. Futrell, *Southampton County Historical Society*

Willie Graham, *Colonial Williamsburg Foundation*

Artelia Green, *Robert R. Moton Memorial Institute*

Julie Gronlund, *Land and Community Associates*

Alice Hanes, *Portsmouth Naval Shipyard Museum*

James N. Haskett, *Colonial National Historical Park*

Jacqueline Hernigle, *Virginia Department of Historic Resources*

James C. Hill, *Virginia Department of Historic Resources*

Margaret D. Holden, *Holley Graded School*

Julian Hudson, *Prestwould Plantation*

Edith Ingram, *Stanton Family Cemetery*

Renee Ingram, *Stanton Family Cemetery*

Harvey N. Johnson, Jr., *Portsmouth*

J. J. Johnson, *Tuskegee University*

Joseph F. Johnston, Jr., *Bremo Plantation*

Daniel P. Jordan, *Thomas Jefferson Memorial Foundation*

Mary Kayaselcuk, *War Memorial Museum of Virginia*

William M. Kelso, *Thomas Jefferson Memorial Foundation*

John R. Kern, *Virginia Department of Historic Resources*

Erika Q. Kinney, *Virginia Union University*

Reverend I. W. Knight, Sr., St. John's A.M.E. Church, Norfolk

Mrs. Bolling Lambeth, *Bedford Historical Society*

Brian C. Little, *Black History Museum and Cultural Center of Virginia*

Lillian W. Lovett, *Newsome House Museum and Cultural Center*

Stephen L. McMaster, *Richmond*

Thomas O. Madden, Jr., *Madden's Tavern*

Mr. and Mrs. Robert F. Marks III, *Belmont Plantation*

Sandra Mayer, *Virginia Department of Historic Resources*

Hugh C. Miller, *Virginia Department of Historic Resources*

Claude V. Moore, *First Calvary Baptist Church, Norfolk*

Jim Nolting, *Saint Paul's College*

Jeffrey M. O'Dell, *Virginia Department of Historic Resources*

Sister Margaret M. O'Rourke, *Sisters of the Blessed Sacrament*

Daniel Perkins, *First African Baptist Church, Richmond*

Margaret T. Peters, *Virginia Department of Historic Resources*

Dan Pezzoni, *Preservation Technologies, Inc.*

Suzette Raney, *Lloyd House, Alexandria*

Lewis Rogers, *Booker T. Washington National Monument*

Emily J. Salmon, *Virginia State Library and Archives*

Hayman Schwartzberg, *Richmond National Battlefield Park*

Kimberly G. Sicola, *Meadow Farm Park*

Wendell C. Sommerville, *Lott Carey Baptist Foreign Mission Convention*

Chauncey Spencer, *Anne Spencer Memorial Foundation*

Howard Stahl, *Berry Hill Plantation*

Lucia C. Stanton, *Thomas Jefferson Memorial Foundation*

Melody Stovall, *Harrison Museum of African-American Culture*

Marc C. Wagner, *Virginia Department of Historic Resources*

Lorena S. Walsh, *Colonial Williamsburg Foundation*

David S. White, *SWA Architects*

Dr. J. L. White, Sr., *First Calvary Baptist Church, Norfolk*

Frances Williams, *Third Street Bethel A.M.E. Church, Richmond*

Mary Louise Williams, *Court Street Baptist Church, Lynchburg*

David Wright, *Lower Bremo Plantation*

The editor also wishes to give special thanks to John S. Salmon, Virginia Department of Historic Resources historian, for providing invaluable editorial assistance.

The Department of Historic Resources gratefully acknowledges the assistance of the Dunlevy Millbank Foundation in supporting the publication of this volume.

The preparation of this volume was financed in part with federal funds from the U.S. Department of the Interior, through the Department of Historic Resources, Commonwealth of Virginia. Under Title VI of the Civil Rights Act of 1964 and Section 504 of the Rehabilitation Act of 1973, the U.S. Department of the Interior prohibits discrimination on the basis of race, color, national origin, or handicap in its federally assisted programs. If you believe that you have been discriminated against in any program or activity described herein, or if you desire further information, please write to: Office of Equal Opportunity, U.S. Department of the Interior, Washington, D.C. 20240. The contents and opinions of this book do not necessarily reflect the views or policies of the Department of the Interior, nor does any mention of trade names or commercial products constitute endorsement or recommendation by the Department of the Interior. The Virginia Department of Historic Resources, in accordance with the Americans with Disabilities Act, will make this publication available in braille, large print, or audio tape upon request. Please allow 4–6 weeks for delivery.

VIRGINIA LANDMARKS OF BLACK HISTORY

SITES ON THE VIRGINIA LANDMARKS REGISTER
AND THE NATIONAL REGISTER OF HISTORIC PLACES

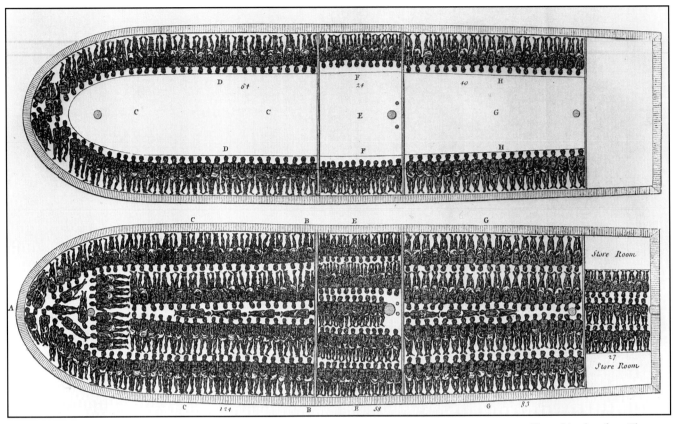

Slave-ship plan, from Thomas Clarkson's History of the Rise, Progress, and Accomplishment of the Slave Trade *(1808).*

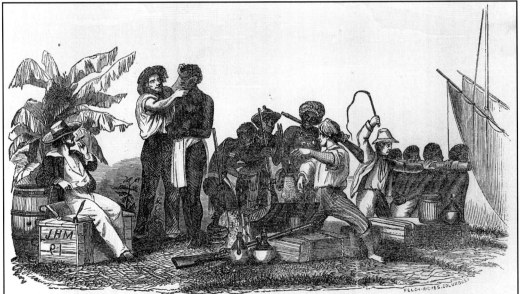

African slave traffic

INTRODUCTION

S INCE 1968 the Department of Historic Resources has listed approximately seventeen hundred buildings, districts, and archaeological sites on the Virginia Landmarks Register and has nominated those same properties to the National Register of Historic Places. So that the register represents the breadth of Virginia's development, a range of historical themes is considered; among them archaeology, architecture, education, entertainment, ethnic heritage, exploration, industry, literature, military affairs, politics, religion, science, and transportation. Within the theme of ethnic heritage, Afro-American history and culture are of particular importance to Virginia.

The black experience in English America began in Virginia with the arrival of the first Africans at Jamestown in August 1619. For nearly four centuries Afro-Americans have constituted an essential part of the Old Dominion's civilization. Although black history is inextricably interwoven with that of Virginia as a whole, many of the structures that housed Afro-Americans and their activities were insubstantial to begin with and have been lost to time. More significantly, for almost two-thirds of the time that blacks have been in Virginia, most existed in a state of servitude and had few opportunities to create a lasting built environment distinctly their own. Nevertheless, despite the scarcity of resources specifically associated with black history, this catalog contains over sixty entries.

Landmarks associated with black history and achievement dating from before the Civil War are especially rare. The Virginia countryside was once dotted with hundreds of slave quarters, but nearly all such structures associated with this most negative side of black life have vanished. The slave housing of the colonial period was so flimsy that architectural historians doubt that any colonial slave quarters other than those of house servants remain. Even the later more substantial slave quarters that resulted from the increased concern for the health of slaves have nearly all disappeared. This catalog includes the three most important of Virginia's handful of surviving slave quarter complexes: Ben Venue, Berry Hill, and Howard's Neck. These quarters, coupled with the planters' residences and the related domestic outbuilding complexes, offer rare glimpses of the landscape of a slave economy. The catalog also singles out an isolated slave dwelling, the late eighteenth-century structure at Prestwould, believed by scholars to be the oldest remaining slave quarter in the Commonwealth.

In a larger sense, of course, most of Virginia's built environment—including almost all of those landmarks constructed before the Civil War—is associated with the story of Virginia's black people, slave and free. Black laborers built Monticello, the James River plantation mansions, and thousands of vernacular houses and related outbuildings. Black craftsmen constructed much of the furniture, built the barns and other outbuildings, erected fences, and labored on the roads that linked Virginia's farms and plantations. Just as the musician interprets the composer's score, so black workers adapted their white masters' designs and directions with the result that the Virginia cultural landscape is as much a black as a white creation. The several score registered plantation dwellings and outbuilding complexes are all landmarks of Virginia's Afro-American history; however, to include all such places in this catalog would dilute the effort to focus on those places specifically identified with the Afro-American story.

The several antebellum landmarks that are represented here are particularly telling relics of the conditions of slavery or highlight noteworthy individuals and events. Two landmarks of the time recall efforts by slaves to free themselves. Meadow Farm in Henrico County figured prominently in the abortive 1800 insurrection of the slave Gabriel. Belmont, in Southampton County, was the site of the suppression of Nat Turner's rebellion in 1831. On a more positive note, Bremo, the famous plantation of General John Hartwell Cocke, is a landmark of one slave owner's efforts to improve the lot of his slaves and to prepare them for freedom.

One of Virginia's most important antebellum landmarks of Afro-American history, and indeed of American history generally, is the birth site of Booker T. Washington in Franklin County where the National Park Service has reconstructed the rude cottage in which he was born. Another noteworthy birth site of the period is that of Lott Cary, the first black missionary to Africa and a founder of the Republic of Liberia, located in Charles City County. A rare relic of antebellum black entrepreneurship is Madden's Tavern in rural Culpeper County, a tavern built, owned, and operated by a free black, Willis Madden.

Although religion was important to Afro-Americans long before the Civil War, early black churches are exceedingly rare. Since any gathering of slaves was suspect, slaves, for the most part, were included in white congregations and attended white churches, where they were confined to slave balconies. The few independent

Loft, Berry Hill slave cabin

black congregations could not assemble to worship unless whites were present. A notable example of an antebellum black church is Third Street Bethel African Methodist Episcopal Church, in Richmond, built in 1857. The Bremo slave chapel, in Fluvanna County is unique as a plantation structure erected by a master specifically to serve the spiritual needs of his slaves.

After emancipation, segregation prevented blacks from sharing leadership and resources, but it also required them to develop their own institutions, many of which have become important historic landmarks. Black colleges, churches, and businesses, created in an atmosphere of prejudice and poverty, were especially remarkable achievements of Virginia's Afro-Americans. Many Afro-Americans

Freed blacks near Richmond, from Harper's Weekly, *1870.*

quickly realized that they would have to depend on their own ingenuity and resources if they were to prosper.

In the decades following the Civil War, the church became perhaps the single most important institution of black life. Congregations built their own houses of worship; a few congregations, primarily urban ones, erected notably large and architecturally distinguished churches within a few decades of emancipation. The Virginia Landmarks Register lists several of these late nineteenth-century works, including Court Street Baptist Church in Lynchburg (1879–80), Fourth Baptist Church in Richmond (1884), St. John's African Methodist Episcopal Church in Norfolk (1887–88), First Baptist Church in Roanoke (1898–1900), and First Baptist Church in Norfolk (1906). Many churches became the social, cultural, and educational centers of black urban life, offering a support system denied blacks by mainstream society.

St. John's A.M.E. Church, Norfolk

The early recognition by freedmen that education was essential to self-sufficiency and economic prosperity resulted in their support of the statewide system of free public education mandated by the Virginia Constitution of 1869. While many conservative whites opposed the new system, some white supporters endowed private primary schools for rural blacks. Two examples on the Virginia Landmarks Register are the Holley Graded School and the Howland Chapel School, both in Northumberland County. Virginia Estelle Randolph, a black primary schoolteacher who was the daughter of former slaves, gained national repute for promoting innovative teaching methods. Her office, now a museum on the grounds of the Virginia Randolph Educational Center in Henrico County, is a National Historic Landmark, a designation given only to places of national significance.

Higher education for blacks initially was limited to industrial and agricultural training schools. Some black leaders, most notably Booker T. Washington, thought that blacks first needed to build a solid economic base consisting of middle-class craftsmen, tradesmen, and farmers, and that training schools were the best means for achieving that goal. Founded in 1868, the earliest and most famous of these schools is Hampton Institute, now the thriving Hampton University. Here Booker T. Washington received his education and formulated the concepts that inspired generations of his fellow blacks. Other training schools, such as Old Christiansburg Industrial Institute, in Montgomery County, and St. Emma's Military Academy on what was formerly Belmead plantation, in Powhatan County, have closed, but their principal buildings remain as landmarks of the movement to equip freedmen and their children with practical skills.

The nation's first state-supported institution of higher education for blacks, Virginia State University, near Petersburg, was established in 1882 to fulfill a campaign promise made to black voters. Virginia Union University, in Richmond, developed from the Richmond Theological School for Freedmen created in 1865; the university was formed in 1896 by merger with other schools. The Episcopal church supported the efforts of the Reverend James Solomon Russell, who in 1883 founded Saint Paul's College in Lawrenceville.

Maggie L. Walker

Taking advantage of their educational opportunities, late nineteenth-century black Virginians surmounted almost overwhelming obstacles to start their own businesses and banks. Their commercial buildings and houses serve to commemorate their achievements. Among these landmarks are the Phoenix Bank of Nansemond in Suffolk, whose founder and first president simultaneously labored as a janitor in a white bank. Nearby in Norfolk stands the Attucks Theatre, designed by Harvey M. Johnson, a black architect, and constructed by blacks. Notable residences include those of the politician and entrepreneur William H. Trusty in Hampton; attorney and newspaper editor J. Thomas Newsome in Newport News; and the nation's first woman bank president, Maggie Lena Walker, in Richmond. Her home is a National Historic Site and is maintained as a museum by the National Park Service. The house is located in Richmond's Jackson Ward Historic District, the most important urban neighborhood in Virginia associated with black enterprise. The district contains some forty blocks of nineteenth and early twentieth-century residential and commercial architecture. It also was the birthplace of one of America's greatest dancers, Bill ("Bojangles") Robinson.

The houses of three blacks who made particularly noteworthy contributions in the twentieth century have been singled out for landmark designation. The Lynch-

Virginia-Cleveland Hall, Hampton University

burg residence of Anne Spencer, lyric poet and civil right spokeswoman, is maintained as a museum. Holly Knoll, the Gloucester County retirement home of Robert Russa Moton, former president of Tuskegee Institute and founder of the National Urban League, has for years been used as a conference center but now faces an uncertain future. The modest Arlington home of Dr. Charles Richard Drew, whose pioneering work in the use of blood plasma helped save thousands of lives in World War II, remains a private residence. Finally, Virginia is fortunate to possess the home of Amaza Lee Meredith, one of the nation's first black woman architects. Azurest South, the stylistically avant-garde house designed as her personal residence, is on the grounds of Virginia State University.

The official recognition of the landmarks of Virginia's Afro-American heritage is an ongoing process of identification and evaluation. The entries in this catalog reflect the efforts of the Department of Historic Resources to focus attention on black history and therefore mark a beginning, not a comprehensive and conclusive listing. In coming years the department and its staff will work with Virginia's citizens to fill the gaps in the record. It is hoped that this catalog will encourage the formal designation of many more landmarks of black history and will serve to increase awareness among all Virginians of the special contributions of Afro-Americans to our history.

EDITOR'S NOTE

The properties covered in this work include all places judged by the department to have significance in Afro-American history that have been listed on the Virginia Landmarks Register or nominated to the National Register of Historic Places before March 1994.

The information in each catalog entry is taken primarily from the research notes and nomination reports filed in the archives of the Department of Historic Resources. Additional information has been provided by department staff members as well as various property owners and property administrators who prepared or reviewed drafts of the entries.

Each entry is followed by the Department of Historic Resources archives file number, a hyphenated number the first part of which is the numerical designation of the city, town, or county in which the place is located. The second part of the number indicates the numerical order in which the place was added to the statewide inventory within the survey of its respective city, town, or county.

A CATALOG OF VIRGINIA LANDMARKS OF BLACK HISTORY

Mary Peake Boulevard

ABERDEEN GARDENS HISTORIC DISTRICT
Hampton

Virginia Landmarks Register, March 10, 1994
National Register of Historic Places, May 26, 1994

Aberdeen Gardens was a New Deal planned community, designed specifically for the resettlement of Afro-American workers of the Newport News and Hampton area, who were living in substandard housing. Begun in 1934 and finished by 1937, this 440-acre subdivision, the only Resettlement Administration community for blacks in Virginia, consisted of 158 single-family homes along with a school and a commercial center, all surrounded by a greenbelt area for subsistence and truck farming. The project, initiated by Hampton Institute (now Hampton University) and funded by the U. S. Department of the Interior's Division of Subsistence Homesteads, later reorganized as the Resettlement Administration, was supervised by Howard University's Hilyard R. Robinson, architect-in-charge, and Jesse R. Otis, program supervisor.

The intent of the undertaking was to design a model for other resettlements of low-income rural and urban blacks. The site chosen was about four miles north of the Newport News business district. Known for its shipbuilding industry and dry-docking facilities, Newport News also supported a large workforce involved in coal shipping. In the mid-thirties most of the 2,500 black workers of this urban-industrial area lived in dilapidated frame houses with no electricity, running water, or central heating. While providing the amenities of modern housing represented a great improvement for these workers, the project went further by proposing a transformation of the residents to a "higher social and health level" (Memorandum, U.S. Department of the Interior, Division of Subsistence Homesteads, March 13, 1935).

The all-encompassing plan was to allow the Aberdeen Gardens residents to experience the benefits of cleanliness, efficiency, and aesthetics in their well-designed housing; maintain gardens on their half-acre lots for self-subsistence, especially during the summer slack months; and profit from the educational opportunities of the Aberdeen Elementary School and adult programs offered by Hampton Institute. The planning, designing, site preparation, and construction were carried out by an all-black workforce. A 1935 press release proudly announced, "This project derives one of its most significant features from the fact that it is a project by Negroes, for Negroes" (ibid.).

The houses were meant to be embodiments of the "local traditional style" united with the best elements from the "modern functional style." A typical house in the subdivision, referred to as a "house-garden" unit, was of brick construction, one-and-a-half stories high, with an attached garage. The plan included a living room, dining and kitchen area, bathroom, and two bedrooms.

Aberdeen Gardens' simple Colonial-styled houses were complemented by the traditional design of Aberdeen Elementary School, an architectural focal point of the project, which was extensively remodeled in 1950. On December 9, 1937, the street names of Aberdeen Gardens were changed from their original alphabetical labels to commemorate well-known recent black leaders.

Aberdeen Gardens received national attention when Eleanor Roosevelt visited it in 1938. The success of the community is evident in the fact that complementary

Moving in, Aberdeen Gardens, 1937

additions to the original area were made during the 1940s and 1950s. Some of the earliest houses have undergone alteration, and the neighborhood today enjoys the many mature shade trees around the houses and on the wide grass boulevard medians. Recognizing that Aberdeen Gardens is a symbol of Afro-American pride, a citizens group of some original homesteaders and their descendants has been formed to protect the integrity of the district and to support its designation as a historic landmark.

114-146

ATTUCKS THEATRE

1008-1012 Church Street, Norfolk

Virginia Landmarks Register, July 21, 1981
National Register of Historic Places, September 16, 1982

A landmark of black popular culture and enterprise, the Attucks Theatre is one of the only theaters in Virginia to be financed, designed, and built exclusively by blacks. Located on Church Street, formerly the main commercial artery of Norfolk's black community, the theater opened in 1919. Its developers were the Twin Cities Amusement Corporation, an organization of black businessmen which operated theaters in both Norfolk and Portsmouth. Its financial backers were the Brown Savings Bank and the Tidewater Trust Company. The architect, Harvey N. Johnson (1892–1973), was one of Virginia's few black architects at the time. Born in Richmond's Jackson Ward, Johnson was educated at Virginia Union University and then Carnegie Institute of Technology in Pittsburgh. At the age of twenty-six, he moved to Norfolk to design and supervise the construction of the Attucks Theatre.

Harvey N. Johnson, Sr.

The Attucks was named for Crispus Attucks, a black man killed in the Boston Massacre of 1770 and traditionally regarded as the first colonist mortally wounded in the American Revolution. Attucks's heroic sacrifice in the struggle for human equality was depicted in the theater's fire curtain, painted with a scene of the Boston Massacre by Lee Lash Studios of New York.

Although segregation in places of public entertainment was not written into law in Virginia until 1926, society in the Old Dominion began moving in that direction much earlier, and the Attucks Theatre symbolizes the black community's attempt to deal with reality. Situated in Norfolk's most concentrated area of black commercial activity and adjacent to a large black residential area, the theater was designed to accommodate shops and professional offices as well as vaudeville productions and motion pictures. With a seating capacity of six hundred, the theater in its heyday received New York's leading black road shows and welcomed entertainers such as Cab Calloway, Bessie Smith, and Ethel Waters. For many of Norfolk's blacks, the Attucks provided their first exposure to the performing arts.

The Great Depression brought on a decline in business activity in the area. The Attucks Theatre closed, and the building was eventually sold to Stark and Legum,

Attucks Theatre

Fire curtain, Attucks Theatre

clothiers, for merchandise storage. Fortunately, except for the removal of the seating, the interior survives without significant alteration, preserving its box seats as well as the painted fire curtain illustrating the death of Crispus Attucks. The theater was targeted for preservation in 1986 and purchased by the Norfolk Redevelopment and Housing Authority. Although it is still being used for storage, the authority hopes that means can be found to rehabilitate the theater for use as a black cultural center.

122-74

AZUREST SOUTH

Virginia State University, Ettrick, Chesterfield County

Virginia Landmarks Register, October 20, 1993
National Register of Historic Places, December 30, 1993

Azurest South was designed by Amaza Lee Meredith (1895–1984), one of the nation's first black female architects, for use as her own residence and studio. The compact dwelling is among the Commonwealth's few mature examples of the International Style, a style developed in Germany following World War I which espoused a complete break with traditional architectural references. Architectural historian Richard Guy Wilson has judged Azurest South to be one of the most advanced residential designs in the state in its day. Meredith's choice of the International Style demonstrated her forward-looking attitude, a rejection of conventional Virginia architecture in favor of the avant-garde.

Following completion of the house in 1939, Meredith lived there with her companion, Dr. Edna Meade Colson, dean of the Virginia State University School of Education, until her death. Born in Lynchburg and trained at Columbia Teachers

Azurest South

Amaza Lee Meredith

College as an artist and teacher, Meredith founded the fine arts department at Virginia State University in 1930. Although principally employed as a teacher, she also enjoyed a limited architectural career, designing houses and interiors for herself, family, and friends in Virginia, Texas, and New York. With Azurest South, Meredith differentiated her principal residence from Azurest North, an enclave of summer cottages she designed for herself and friends in Sag Harbor, New York.

Picturesquely sited in a tree-framed landscaped lawn adjacent to the VSU campus, Azurest South is Meredith's most developed architectural work. Like Thomas Jefferson's Monticello, Azurest South is an instance where architect and client were one and the same, and like Monticello, Azurest South demonstrated a fascination with modernity, a familiarity with new materials and construction details, and a love of nature. Features characteristic of the International Style employed at Azurest South include the stuccoed surfaces devoid of applied ornament, the curved corners accented with bands of glass block, the metal windows, and the flat roof, all blended into a carefully massed asymmetrical composition. Meredith's interest in an African-American aesthetic is reflected in the tile surfaces she designed for the kitchen, vivid geometric compositions of red, black, pink, and green. The bathroom is also a remarkable demonstration of an interest in color and new materials with its black and celery-colored carrara-glass surfaces. Her interest in African-American expressions is further reflected in a metal bas-relief frieze set into the wall of what was originally her studio. The frieze, titled "My Lady's Boudoir," depicting stylized black women, was executed in the 1940s by Cecilia Scott, one of her students.

At her death Meredith left a half interest in the property to the Virginia State University National Alumni Association. The association purchased the remaining interest in Azurest South from Dr. Colson's estate following her death in 1986. The property is now used for alumni association meetings and social functions.

333-62-36

Living room, Azurest South

Banneker SW-9 boundary stone

BANNEKER SW-9 INTERMEDIATE BOUNDARY STONE

Eighteenth and Van Buren Streets, Arlington County

Virginia Landmarks Register, February 15, 1977
National Historic Landmark, May 11, 1976

One of the original forty boundary stones, this sandstone marker, one foot square and standing only fifteen inches high, was set in 1792 to mark the westernmost point of the District of Columbia. The district's boundaries as well as its streets and public buildings were surveyed by Major Andrew Ellicott. He was assisted by Benjamin Banneker (also spelled Bannaker), a black mathematician, scientist, and surveyor. Banneker's involvement with the siting of the federal city made him one of the most famous Afro-Americans of his time, although he achieved widespread recognition for his other accomplishments as well.

Benjamin Banneker (1731–1806) spent most of his life in Baltimore County, Maryland, where his ancestors had settled in the seventeenth century. His grandfather, reputedly an African prince named Bannke or Bannaka, was married to a former indentured servant Englishwoman named Molly Welsh who taught the young Banneker. He also received some instruction at a Quaker school. Despite his limited formal education, Banneker became proficient in mathematics and astronomy. In 1792 he compiled an almanac for which he produced all the mathematical and astronomical calculations. The almanac drew the attention of many men of science including the marquis de Condorcet, secretary of the Academy of Science in Paris, and Major Ellicott, an astute astronomer as well as surveyor. Bannaker's almanacs, one of the first series of almanacs printed in the United States, went through twenty-six editions. Contained in the almanac were his suggestions for the formation of a department of the interior and a league of nations. Banneker was also interested in nature, and his observations of natural phenomenon led him to the conclusion that locusts swarmed in seventeen-year cycles. Banneker became an early advocate of civil rights when he requested Thomas Jefferson to use his influence to end official prejudice against blacks.

Banneker's personal records were destroyed when his home burned on the day of his funeral. The SW-9 Intermediate Boundary Stone has thus come to symbolize the achievements of this gifted individual who was viewed as an example of the ability of the black race during a time when even the most educated whites were skeptical of blacks' intellectual competence.

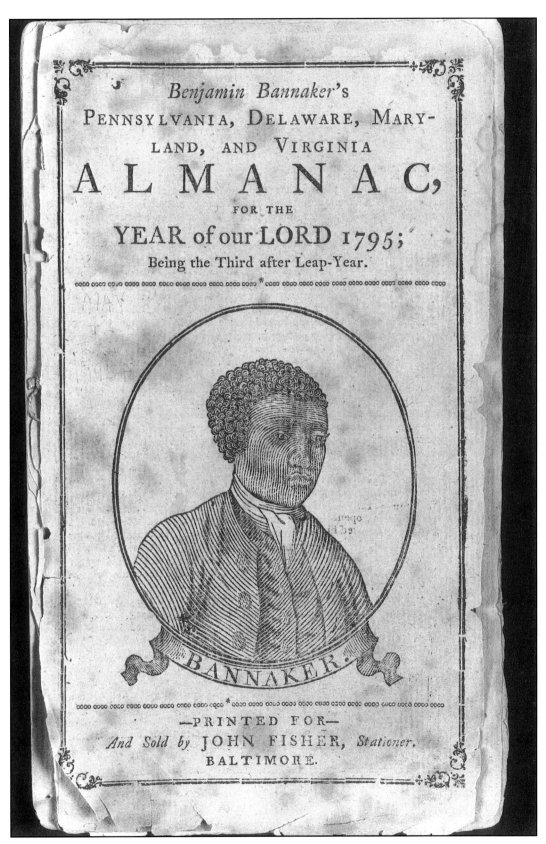

Benjamin Banneker

Bedford Historic Meeting House

Bedford Historic Meeting House, circa 1897

BEDFORD HISTORIC MEETING HOUSE

153 West Main Street, Bedford

Virginia Landmarks Register, September 20, 1977
National Register of Historic Places, January 31, 1978

The Bedford Historic Meeting House represents one of the efforts made by small towns in Virginia to accommodate the religious and educational needs of blacks in the decades following the Civil War. The building was erected in 1838 to house the Bedford County seat's first Methodist church. By 1886 the Methodists had outgrown the little brick church and left it for a larger building. Leading local white citizens, interested in the welfare of their former slaves, were instrumental in having the building purchased by the Episcopalians. In 1886 the building was reconsecrated St. Philip's Episcopal Church, a mission church serving Bedford's black Episcopalians.

Typical of rural areas in Virginia in the late nineteenth century, educational facilities for blacks were almost nonexistent in Bedford County. Thus St. Philip's congregation erected a two-story frame annex on the rear of the church to serve as a day school for the children of the parish. This simple school remained in use until a segregated public school was established to serve the area's blacks. The Reverend Scott Wood, the rector of St. Philip's who was responsible for the founding of the St. Philip's school, later became a principal of Saint Paul's Polytechnic Institute (later Saint Paul's College), an Episcopal training school for blacks in Lawrenceville.

As segregated facilities were abolished in the 1950s and 1960s, St. Philip's congregation merged with Bedford's white Episcopal congregation in 1968. The church building, the oldest in the city of Bedford, fell into disrepair and was slated for demolition. The Bedford Historical Society was formed as an emergency group to purchase and preserve the church as a local landmark. The society was successful in raising funds to purchase the building and took title in 1969. The church's name was then officially changed to the Bedford Historic Meeting House. A fire destroyed the schoolhouse annex in 1977 but left the original portion of the church without significant damage. It has since been handsomely restored for use as the society's meeting place and location for community events.

The Bedford Historic Meeting House is architecturally related to a number of antebellum brick houses of worship scattered from Bedford to southwest Virginia. These simple Greek Revival structures all have the temple form with pedimented gable ends. Nearly all have a square belfry with paired pilasters framing the corners and a low, plain spire. Unlike the others, the Bedford meetinghouse was built with a side door, intended for the use of slaves to reach the stair to the gallery. The side door, as well as the stair and slave gallery, survives.

141-05

BELMEAD
(ST. EMMA'S MILITARY ACADEMY)

Powhatan Vicinity, Powhatan County

Virginia Landmarks Register, May 13, 1969
National Register of Historic Places, November 17, 1969

In 1893 Colonel and Mrs. Edward de Vaux Morrell of Philadelphia purchased Belmead, a large plantation on the James River in Powhatan County, to establish a school for black youth. The Gothic Revival mansion designed in 1845 by New York architect Alexander Jackson Davis for Philip St. George Cocke, son of General John Hartwell Cocke of Bremo, formed the nucleus of the plantation.

Colonel Edward de Vaux Morrell

Louise Drexel Morrell

In their decision to become patrons of black education, the Morrells apparently were influenced by Mrs. Morrell's half sister, Mother M. Katharine Drexel. Born into a rich and socially prominent Philadelphia Catholic family, Mother Katharine in 1889 decided to forgo wealth and rank and enter religious life. With the support of the archbishop of Philadelphia, she founded the order of the Sisters of the Blessed Sacrament to serve the religious and educational needs of Indians and blacks.

Like Mother Katharine, Colonel Morrell was especially concerned with equipping black youth for independence and self-sufficiency in post–Civil War America. By placing emphasis on practical skills, his approach was similar to that of Booker T. Washington. In a letter written in June 1925, Morrell stated that the school he planned at Belmead was "never founded to impart 'higher education' but to give deserving young men an opportunity to become good intelligent mechanics or agriculturists" (*Powhatan Today,* January 24, 1991). Named St. Emma's Industrial and Agricultural School for Emma Bouvier Drexel, Mrs. Morrell's mother, the school opened in 1895 and admitted only boys of African descent from the South. The first graduate, John Paul Scott, received his diploma from Mrs. Morrell in 1899.

The school flourished and soon was open to students from every part of the country. All students were required to take military training. Classes in numerous trades were offered including blacksmithing, wagon building, automobile repair, carpentry, cooking, tailoring, masonry, and upholstering. Agricultural training was also an important part of the curriculum. In 1919 St. Emma's military program received official ROTC status from the War Department. The school was later renamed St. Emma's Military Academy and came under the administration of the Holy Ghost Fathers, a Catholic order. Academic training became an increasingly important part of the program.

During its seventy-seven years of operation, St. Emma's graduated approximately ten thousand young men. Its program blending practical skills with academic high school education and military instruction received national recognition among blacks. Ironically, because of the school's self-sufficiency and isolation, it was little known among the general public of Virginia.

The civil rights movement of the 1960s, coupled with school desegregation, led to a dwindling of interest in attending an all-black, all-male, church-affiliated military school. Enrollment dropped, and the school closed in 1972. Its custodians, the Sisters of the Blessed Sacrament, ordered the demolition of all the school buildings except the Belmead mansion. In 1987 Belmead was leased by the sisters for use as a Catholic high school.

St. Emma's band, Belmead, circa 1900

BELMONT

Capron Vicinity, Southampton County

Virginia Landmarks Register, July 17, 1973
National Register of Historic Places, October 3, 1973

The Nat Turner insurrection, the bloodiest and best-known slave revolt in American history, was suppressed at Belmont on the morning of August 23, 1831. Turner, a black slave born in 1800, believed himself divinely appointed to lead his people out of bondage. He raised a band of followers and planned to kill every white person in their path as they endeavored to capture the Southampton County seat, Jerusalem. Upon the ruins of the white man's civilization Turner intended to establish a Negro republic where runaway slaves and free blacks could build a new life.

The revolt began on Sunday night, August 21, 1831. Beginning at the Travis place, home of his owner, Turner and about seventy followers proceeded from house to house, killing some sixty people in all. They had covered about fifteen miles by the early morning of August 23 when they approached Belmont, home of Dr. Samuel Blunt. Warned of the massacre the day before, Dr. Blunt assembled his slaves and gave them the choice of defending the plantation or joining the insurgents. Blunt's slaves unanimously chose to defend their master and armed themselves with picks and hoes, perhaps because Blunt also had at hand family and friends armed with rifles. Upon reaching Belmont, Turner and his band (by then reduced by casualties and desertions to about twenty) were ambushed. Several of his men were killed, including Hark Travis, Turner's chief lieutenant. The rest dispersed and eventually were captured or killed. Twenty of the rebellious slaves subsequently were executed.

Nat Turner

Turner escaped and remained in hiding until he was apprehended on October 30. While being held in the county jail, Nat Turner made his famous confessions to Thomas R. Gray, his counsel. They were published before the end of the year and widely distributed. Sentenced to death, Turner was hanged November 11, 1831.

Although the revolt was suppressed, no other event spread such a fear of blacks, both slave and free, through Virginia and the rest of the South. The aftermath was a series of actions designed to keep slaves helpless and submissive. Any sentiment toward emancipation was seen as a dangerous threat to the general security. Laws were enacted in Virginia and other southern states to prohibit slave education and to stifle their practice of religion because religious conviction was seen as a motivating force for Turner. Free blacks were also greatly restricted, and the American Colonization Society received much support for sending them, as well as slaves prepared for freedom, to Liberia. Although other revolts would follow, Nat Turner's insurrection effectively demonstrated the futility of any expectation that blacks could obtain their freedom by armed resistance. Despite its failure, the uprising and subsequent suppression of blacks succeeded in making slavery the chief national issue, an issue which eventually had to be settled by civil war.

87-30

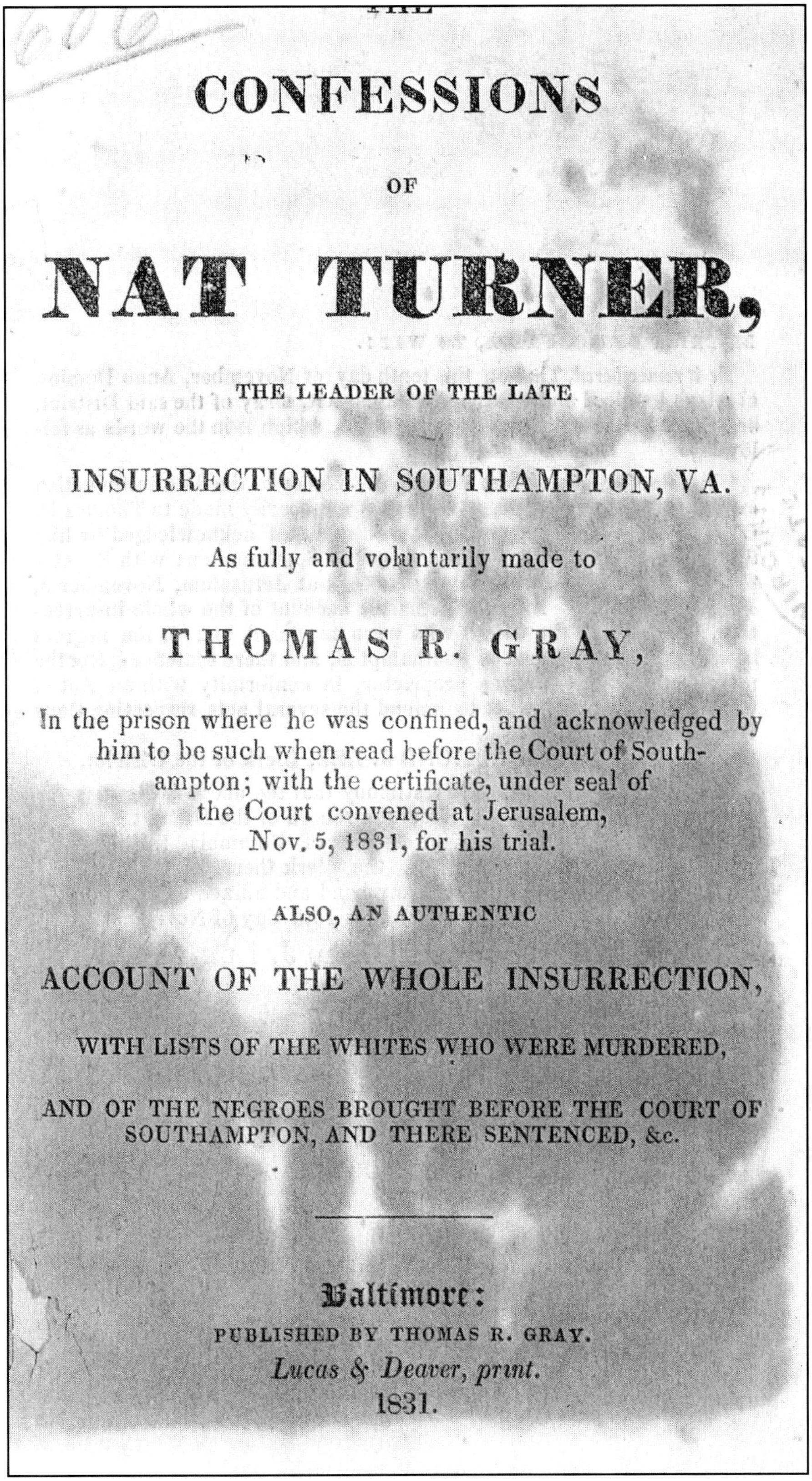

CONFESSIONS

OF

NAT TURNER,

THE LEADER OF THE LATE

INSURRECTION IN SOUTHAMPTON, VA.

As fully and voluntarily made to

THOMAS R. GRAY,

In the prison where he was confined, and acknowledged by
him to be such when read before the Court of Southampton; with the certificate, under seal of
the Court convened at Jerusalem,
Nov. 5, 1831, for his trial.

ALSO, AN AUTHENTIC

ACCOUNT OF THE WHOLE INSURRECTION,

WITH LISTS OF THE WHITES WHO WERE MURDERED,

AND OF THE NEGROES BROUGHT BEFORE THE COURT OF
SOUTHAMPTON, AND THERE SENTENCED, &c.

Baltimore:
PUBLISHED BY THOMAS R. GRAY.
Lucas & Deaver, print.
1831.

Title page, The Confessions of Nat Turner

Ben Venue slave quarters

BEN VENUE

Ben Venue, Rappahannock County

Virginia Landmarks Register, October 16, 1979
National Register of Historic Places, December 28, 1979

The Ben Venue slave quarters tangibly illustrate a change in attitude toward slave housing which occurred in the early nineteenth century. In the previous century, especially during the colonial period, slaves in Virginia, and indeed throughout the southern colonies, were regarded almost as livestock. Their quarters generally were little more than rude shacks with wooden chimneys and without windows or floors. In many cases the quarters of field hands, as opposed to house servants, were located out of sight from the master's residence, usually in the woods where they could not clutter the view. The flimsy quality of this early chattel sheltering has thwarted preservation; no slave quarters in Virginia have been positively identified as belonging to the colonial period.

By the second decade of the nineteenth century, pride of land ownership came to be reflected in the layout of some of the more prosperous plantations. Planning was estate-oriented; the various plantation buildings were designed to form a unified complex rather than a scattering of strictly utilitarian units. Also, because slaves were a valuable commodity, their owners took a greater interest in their

Ben Venue owner's residence

well-being, realizing that crude housing did not enhance health and productivity.

At Ben Venue, a fifteen-hundred-acre plantation established by William V. Fletcher in 1844, the main house, service outbuildings, and slave quarters were visually unified through their architectural treatment. Like the main house, the ancillary structures are brick buildings with corbeled brick cornices and distinctive parapet gable ends with corbeled shoulders. The three slave quarters, instead of being hidden away, are conspicuously located lining a ridge in a field in front of the main house. Each of these compact, single-room dwellings is a solidly built structure with a stone foundation, glazed windows, and an exterior-end brick chimney. They even retain traces of original penciled (white-painted) mortar joints. Although the exteriors made for interesting eye-catchers from the main house, the interiors were still relatively spartan with rough floors and ladder stairs.

Despite their simplicity the Ben Venue slave quarters form probably the most architecturally sophisticated grouping of slave quarters surviving in Virginia. They, along with the rest of the brick buildings in the plantation complex, are attributed to James Leake Powers, a master mason whom local tradition credits with constructing numerous buildings in the area, particularly in Washington, the county seat. Ben Venue is located in one of the most scenic areas of Virginia, with panoramic views of verdant rolling hills and the Blue Ridge Mountains. The quarters are thus a reminder that the institution of slavery penetrated well into the nation's gentler landscape, far removed from the harsh environment of the Deep South, the setting more frequently associated with slavery.

78-3

BERRY HILL

South Boston Vicinity, Halifax County

Virginia Landmarks Register, November 5, 1968
National Register of Historic Places, November 25, 1969
National Historic Landmark, November 11, 1971

Berry Hill, the great Greek Revival mansion completed in 1842 for the planter and entrepreneur James Coles Bruce, is the nucleus of what once was one of Virginia's largest and most prosperous plantations, an agricultural landscape dependent on the toil of Afro-Americans. Many of the antebellum components of this vast estate survive and offer an exceptional view of slave life and labor. Here the relationship between master and servant is vividly symbolized by the templelike house dominating the surrounding outbuildings, quarters, and fields, a structure which lent its occupants the aura of deities governing the lives of their charges.

Blacks were working the Berry Hill lands at least as early as 1803 when the prop-

Servants' bells, Berry Hill

erty was assembled by Isaac Coles. In 1814 Coles bequeathed what was then referred to as the Dan River plantation, together with sixty-nine slaves, to his
nephew Edward C. Carrington. The foundations of several early nineteenth-century slave quarters remain visible at Berry Hill today.

Following James Coles Bruce's purchase of the plantation in 1841, numerous
other buildings and structures were erected with slave labor to accommodate
plantation activity. In addition to the mansion, Bruce had many stone slave quarters constructed, quarters that were unusually substantial for their time. Two of
the quarters stand essentially intact while the ruins of five others remain. Among
the farm buildings of this period is a granary housing what is probably a unique
surviving privy to serve field hands. The privy was outfitted with doors and stalls,
as well as a separate entrance for the overseer, to satisfy the emerging Victorian
sense of modesty.

Bruce also operated a stone quarry at Berry Hill, near which are the sites of sev-

Slave house, Berry Hill

Slave house interior, Berry Hill

eral quarters for the slave stonecutters. The stone obtained here was used by slaves not only for the quarters but for architectural details on the mansion and for extensive walls and culverts throughout the plantation; many of these features survive. An especially significant feature relating to Afro-American culture is the Berry Hill slave cemetery, one of the largest recorded in Virginia. The cemetery contains the graves of well over two hundred individuals, each with a rough, uninscribed granite headstone and footstone. Bruce family memoirs note that during the Reconstruction era the plantation carpenter constructed coffins for the blacks still living on the plantation.

The role of domestic slaves tending the mansion is illustrated by the long service wing containing servants' quarters, kitchen, laundry, and an intact servants' privy at the end. Close by are several outbuildings including an unusually large smokehouse and icehouse. Inside the mansion is a complete set of servants' bells, believed to be the only complete surviving antebellum set in Virginia. The bells, mounted on springs, were linked by long wires to pulls in individual rooms; each bell sounded a different pitch.

Ongoing archaeological and architectural research and examination of the property are likely to lead to the discovery of additional sites and structures related to slave activities. These Berry Hill sites hold great potential for significant information on Afro-American material culture and Virginia slave life.

41-4

Upper Bremo

BREMO HISTORIC DISTRICT

Bremo Bluff, Fluvanna County

Virginia Landmarks Register, September 9, 1969
National Register of Historic Places, November 17, 1969
National Historic Landmark, November 11, 1971

The Bremo Historic District includes the three estates created by the planter, sol-
dier, and reformer General John Hartwell Cocke (1780–1866), a leading opponent
of slavery. The focal point of the district is Upper Bremo, the Palladian-style
mansion completed in 1820 as General Cocke's principal residence on the plantation. Still preserved in its west wing is the schoolroom in which Cocke undertook
the education of his slaves. A poignant reminder of Cocke's compassion and interest in the welfare of the people for whom he felt great responsibility, the room
even preserves the original benches on which his slaves sat for their lessons. Also
on the plantation is one of the unusual slave houses Cocke had built of pisé, or
rammed-earth construction, which he declared to be "the warmest shelter in winter and the coolest in the summer" (Cocke to James Skinner, June 4, 1821, *American
Farmer* 3 [August 19, 1821]).

General John Hartwell Cocke

Bremo slave schoolroom

One of the few members of the Virginia aristocracy openly to express contempt for slavery, General Cocke in 1832 wrote to Joseph C. Cabell: "I have long & still steadfastly believe that Slavery is the great cause of all the chief evils of our land, individual as well as national" (Martin Boyd Coyner, Jr., *John Hartwell Cocke of Bremo: Agriculture and Slavery in the Ante-Bellum South*). Despite his opposition to the institution, Cocke did not believe slaves should be immediately emancipated. The majority of slaves were uneducated and inexperienced in personal responsibility, and Cocke felt they would be victimized if they were not adequately prepared for freedom. He demonstrated his conviction by educating his own slaves, employing a young white woman to teach them the three Rs within his own house. In 1831, when the Commonwealth outlawed the employment of white people to teach blacks, Cocke's wife continued the effort and was assisted by several of their own by-now literate slaves. Some of the illustrated posters used to teach the young blacks reading and moral values are preserved by Cocke's descendants.

General Cocke's concern for slaves extended well beyond his own plantation. He became one of the earliest vice-presidents of the American Colonization Society, an organization dedicated to establishing a republic of freedmen in Africa, in what was to become Liberia. Cocke realized that only the ablest slaves should settle in Liberia, he freed to go there those of is own slaves who possessed sufficient skills and education. Their gratitude was expressed in the many letters they sent back to Bremo. Some letters also expressed dismay at conditions in Liberia. Cocke further attempted to equip slaves for emigration by establishing a demonstration plantation in Alabama where slaves could work to buy their freedom as well as learn sufficient skills to live a successful and rewarding life following resettlement.

Noble in intent, General Cocke's opposition to slavery and his efforts to prepare blacks for freedom inspired few imitators among his peers, so fearful were they of the consequences of upsetting the established order. Cocke lived to see the Civil War be the violent cure for what he described as "the cancer eating upon the vitals of the Commonwealth" (Coyner). His beautiful house overlooking the James River stands today not only as an architectural landmark but as a monument to an individual who sought vainly for constructive solutions to an evil institution.

32-2

BREMO SLAVE CHAPEL

Bremo Bluff, Fluvanna County

Virginia Landmarks Register, December 18, 1979
National Register of Historic Places, March 17, 1980

The simple Gothic Revival structure at Bremo Bluff now serving as the parish hall of Grace Episcopal Church originally was the slave chapel for Bremo, the adjacent plantation of General John Hartwell Cocke. It is the state's only known slave chapel and represents Cocke's deep concern for the religious and moral edification of slaves. Realizing that slavery eventually would be abolished, Cocke felt southern leaders such as himself should prepare their slaves for the future. He illegally taught his slaves to read and strongly believed that it was his Christian duty to provide them with religious instruction. Cocke held firmly that slave literacy was essential for effectively conveying the message of Christianity and all its moral implications.

General Cocke determined that his slaves should have an edifice for the sole purpose of worship. He thus had this board-and-batten structure erected in 1835 at Lower Bremo, one of the plantation's three main sections. Following its completion, he invited his young missionary friend, Cortlandt Van Rensselaer, of New York, to dedicate it. Van Rensselaer had come to Bremo in 1833 at Cocke's request to perform missionary work among the blacks. The ceremony was attended by members of the Cocke family, their friends, and nearly all of the Bremo slaves. Upon hearing of the chapel's construction, Peyton Skipwith, one of Bremo's former slaves, who had been given his freedom to live in Liberia, wrote to Cocke's niece: "I was happy to hear that Master has bilt a church for the cullard people. I know that they enjoy themselves better than they would hear [here]" (John C. Maple, "History of Bremo Parish Church," MS in VDHR Archives).

Several months after the dedication, Van Rensselaer moved to Halifax County and wrote, "As there is already a light burning on the banks of the James, I must try hard as may be the task—to be instrumental on kindling up another on the Roanoke" (ibid.). After that, Cocke had difficulty finding suitable people to lead his slaves' religious activities. Services were held in the chapel as regularly as possible up to the Civil War, however, with Cocke or his wife, Louisa, frequently conducting the services themselves. Cocke further demonstrated his conviction by taking communion in Richmond's African Baptist Church in 1852.

The chapel fell into disuse after the Civil War. In 1884 the Cocke family offered the building to the community of Bremo Bluff to serve as an Episcopal church. That same year the building was moved from Lower Bremo's chapel field (as it is still known) to Bremo Bluff and was consecrated as Grace Church. Services were held in the building until 1924 when a new brick church was built. The chapel was moved again, a short distance to the north, to make way for the new church and was converted to a parish hall. It required extensive repair when a large tree fell across it the next year. Following rehabilitation, the former slave chapel has continued in use as a parish hall to the present.

32-30

POMPEY CALLAWAY HOUSE

Elliston, Montgomery County

Virginia Landmarks Register, June 20, 1989
National Register of Historic Places, November 13, 1989
(The Pompey Callaway house is included in the multiple property nomination
"The Prehistoric and Historic Resources of Montgomery County")

This 1910 house in the historically black section of the town of Elliston is the individual architectural expression of a former slave working with traditional forms and building practices. Pompey Callaway was born a slave in Franklin County. The Callaway name comes from his owner, and tradition holds that Callaway was a nephew of his master. His Franklin County origins apparently made a strong impression on Pompey Callaway for his Elliston house is said to have been modeled on the home of his former master. This would explain why a house completed in 1910 has the appearance of one normally dating from the late antebellum period.

In planning his house Pompey Callaway employed the three-bay, center-passage, single-room-deep format known as the I house, a house type employed for many Virginia vernacular dwellings from the mid-eighteenth century on. The semiexterior end chimneys on Callaway's home are also an early form. Such chimneys are found frequently on brick houses of Virginia's piedmont and southwest sections dating from the early nineteenth century. Interestingly, although Callaway's chimneys follow a traditional form, the house is more up-to-date than it would appear because the chimneys do not serve fireplaces but are used to carry stove flues. Other archaic features are the basement openings, treated here as vents with vertical iron bars rather than as glazed windows. Likewise, the entrance with its sidelights and transom could easily be mistaken for an entrance of the antebellum period.

Although Callaway was employed as a station worker in Elliston, he was clearly skilled in the building trades. Not only did he undertake the actual construction of his house, he made his own bricks. He crushed and tempered the clay and shale in his own pug mill or "horsemill." Nightly he drew water for the process from a forty-foot well. He molded the bricks by hand and fired them in a kiln near the house. The brickwork is laid in seven-course American bond rather than faced with brick veneer, then coming into common use.

The structure took many years to complete because most of Callaway's labor on the house was confined to weekends. Callaway's pride in his personal heritage resulted in one of the most substantial black-owned houses in the county dating from the early twentieth century. Except for a modern one-story rear addition, the house has survived with practically no alterations.

60-434

CARTER'S GROVE

Williamsburg Vicinity, James City County

Virginia Landmarks Register, September 9, 1969
National Register of Historic Places, November 17, 1969
National Historic Landmark, April 15, 1970

For most of its history, the James River plantation Carter's Grove has been noted primarily for its stately Georgian mansion, one of the nation's most sophisticated examples of colonial architecture. Built for Carter Burwell, grandson of Robert ("King") Carter, the grand brick dwelling with its outstanding woodwork was the focal point for one of the most important Virginia plantations of the colonial era.

Since its acquisition by the Colonial Williamsburg Foundation in the 1960s

Carter's Grove has been exhibited chiefly as a museum of high-style architecture and aristocratic lifeways. In the 1970s however, archaeological excavation discovered the site of the Burwell farm quarter, which was probably occupied by some twenty slaves at the end of the colonial period. This discovery led to the determination that the broader aspects of plantation life should be interpreted at Carter's Grove. To this end, the Colonial Williamsburg Foundation, over the following decade, carried out extensive documentary research and fieldwork throughout the state on buildings associated with slavery. The highly visible result of this effort is the re-created Carter's Grove quarter, assembled in 1989 using eighteenth-century construction techniques.

This visualization of a lost landscape is the stage for one of the most visited interpretations of slave life offered by an American museum. The foundation's exhi-

Carter's Grove slave quarters

bition is increasingly focusing on the slaves of the area, slaves whose group—if not individual—identities can be discovered. Recent research has shown that forebears of some of the Carter's Grove slaves had lived and worked in the area since the 1660s, and others were brought from present-day eastern Nigeria or western Cameroon in the 1720s. By the middle of the eighteenth century, many of the Carter's Grove slaves had ties to several hundred slaves living on Burwell family farms in the immediate neighborhood.

Archaeological and documentary research has shown that the Carter's Grove slaves selectively adapted elements from their mixed African and Virginia heritage to create a unique Afro-American culture in their quarters. The foundation's current interpretation of the plantation slave life focuses on the richness and complexity of that culture, with emphasis on the few material goods that most slaves possessed.

The stability of the Carter's Grove slave community depended on the profitability of tobacco agriculture in the tidewater. When, in the last quarter of the century, the Burwells decided their future was on the frontier, most members of the slave community were forced to move to western Virginia. Though Carter's Grove's villagelike aspect gradually disappeared, the modern re-creation of the slave quarters serves an important reminder of the dependence of Virginia's colonial aristocracy on slave labor to sustain its lifestyle.

47-1

LOTT CARY BIRTH SITE

Charles City Vicinity, Charles City County

Virginia Landmarks Register, May 20, 1980
National Register of Historic Places, July 30, 1980

For more than a century and a half, this late eighteenth-century vernacular dwelling has been recognized by the black community of Charles City County as the birthplace of Lott Cary (1780–1829), the first black American missionary to Africa and one of the founding fathers of Liberia. (His surname Cary is also sometimes spelled Carey.) The modest house and its rustic setting are the only visible remnants of the plantation belonging to John Bowry, on which Cary was born a slave. Cary lived here until 1804 when his master hired him out to the owner of a Richmond tobacco warehouse. Although he remained a slave, removal to the city offered Cary far more promise for acting on personal initiative than was possible in the countryside. Under the direction of Baptist preacher John Courtney, Cary publicly declared himself a Christian in 1807 and became a member of the First Baptist Church of Richmond. He taught himself to read and write soon after his conversion by memorizing verses of the New Testament.

Cary's speed and accuracy in dispatching tobacco hogsheads earned him a promotion to supervisor of tobacco hands. Using bonuses as well as profits gained from selling waste tobacco, he accumulated $850 with which he purchased freedom for himself and his children in 1813. That same year Cary qualified for the Baptist ministry.

In 1815 Cary and a colleague, Collin Teague, were instrumental in founding the African Missionary Society. Cary also became active in the American Colonization Society, which succeeded in planting a small colony of free blacks on the west coast of Africa in 1819. With support from the American Baptist Board of Foreign Missions, Cary and a small band of Virginia free blacks sailed for the Liberian coast in 1821. When asked why he would give up a comfortable existence for the unknown, Cary replied: "I am an African, and in this country, however meritorious my conduct, and respectable my character, I cannot receive credit due to either. I wish to go to a country where I shall be estimated by my merits, not by my complexion; and I fell bound to labor for my suffering race" (Ralph Randolph Gurley, *Life of Jehudi Ashmun, Late Colonial Agent in Liberia*).

Cary began his missionary work by founding the Providence Baptist Church of Monrovia. He also helped to establish native schools. Throughout his ministry he worked equally hard to make the struggling colony of Liberia a going concern. He died in a gunpowder explosion in 1829, unaware that he had been elected to succeed the late Jehudi Ashmun as governor of the colony. The town of Careysburg in Liberia in named in his honor.

18-61

Lott Cary

Court Street Baptist Church

COURT STREET BAPTIST CHURCH

Court and Sixth Streets, Lynchburg

Virginia Landmarks Register, June 16, 1981
National Register of Historic Places, July 8, 1982

Court Street Baptist Church is the mother church of Lynchburg's black Baptists and is the most conspicuous historic landmark of the city's Afro-American heritage. When completed in 1880, it was the largest church building in the city, and its spire was the tallest object on the downtown skyline. The congregation was organized in 1843, when the city's black Baptists officially separated from the parent First Baptist Church. The group met in a converted theater provided by the parent church until it was destroyed by fire in 1858. It was known as the African Baptist Church of Lynchburg and, in accordance with the law, had white pastors until after the Civil War. After the fire the congregation moved to a remodeled tobacco factory near the site of the present building. That building was replaced in 1867 by a new church that in turn was demolished in 1879 following a panic there the previous autumn. A false alarm that the balconies were collapsing during a crowded wedding resulted in eight people being trampled to death.

Much opposition arose among Lynchburg's white citizens when word got out that the black Baptists intended to purchase a lot on the corner of Court and Sixth streets, near their former church, and erect an impressive new edifice. There had been no objection to a black church being in a fashionable neighborhood during antebellum times as it meant that whites could keep their servants in close proximity and monitor their loyalty. However, following the Civil War whites preferred that the freed blacks move their church elsewhere. The black Baptists were determined to stay in the area. Attempts to prevent them from purchasing the Court Street property by making it difficult for them to borrow money failed when the members contributed enough not only to purchase the lot but to cover much of the construction cost. The church was able to obtain the funds so expeditiously because its members distrusted white-run banks and kept their savings hidden in their homes.

Selected to design the church was the locally prominent white architect R. C. Burkholder. Black labor alone accomplished its construction, decoration, and furnishings. White opposition to the project softened as the building went up. Shortly before its dedication, the local press praised the work: "With its tall and symmetrical spire pointing silently but unmistakenly heavenward, it stands an almost imperishable monument to the vigor, enterprise and religious zeal of the society to which it belongs" (undated clipping in Charles M. Blackford scrapbook, Jones Memorial Library, Lynchburg).

Burkholder's graceful though straightforward design remains little altered to the present although the spire was damaged by a storm in 1993 and is awaiting re-construction. The interior is lighted by its original vividly colored stained-glass windows manufactured by William Hefferman of Lynchburg. The huge original gasolier, now electrified, still dominates the ceiling. The gallery retains the Carl Barckhoff pipe organ installed in 1899. The church itself continues to house a large and active congregation.

118-156

DOUGLASS HIGH SCHOOL
(DOUGLASS COMMUNITY SCHOOL)

408 East Market Street, Leesburg, Loudoun County

Virginia Landmarks Register, October 9, 1991
National Register of Historic Places, September 24, 1992

Leesburg's Douglass High School is a significant reminder of the determination of Virginia's Afro-Americans to receive a good secondary education in good facilities. Until the end of segregated public education, blacks encountered enormous obstacles in obtaining schools that even remotely approached the quality of those for white children. Black citizens frequently had to rely on their own initiative to get the schools to which they felt entitled; local and state government frequently made only a feeble effort. Such was the case in Loudoun County in the 1930s. Before the construction of the Douglass High School, black high school students attended

Douglass High School class of 1947

the Loudoun County Training School, an antiquated frame structure with notably unsafe conditions. The curriculum was sparse, and the school was not accredited with the state of Virginia. There was no equipment for laboratory science and home economic classes; these classes thus were not offered.

An effort to improve the situation was launched in the late 1930s when the parent/teacher associations of various black schools in the county formed the County-Wide League. The league's goal was to purchase land on which a modern high school could be built. The members raised funds by holding bake sales, rummage sales, dances, ball games, and other events. Sufficient money was obtained by 1939, and an eight-acre site was acquired. In 1940 the league sold the site to the Loudoun County school board for $1. The county's efforts to borrow construction funds from the State Literary Fund met such discouragement that the County-Wide

League hired Charles H. Houston of Washington, D.C., an attorney active in civil rights cases, to represent it in persuading the county to find the money to build the school. With both patience and persistence, the league succeeded in 1941 in obtaining a loan of $30,000 from the State Literary Fund for the county. The new high school, named for the former slave and noted abolitionist Frederick Douglass, was opened that same year. Even then, the school board provided only the barest necessities; the blacks had to raise money themselves for various furnishings and other equipment including chairs for the auditorium, laboratory equipment, a piano, equipment for the home economics department, and band instruments. Douglass High School was eventually accredited and remained the only place in the county where blacks could attend high school until the desegregation of the public school system in 1968.

The existence of Douglass High School made the attainment of higher levels of education a possibility for many of the county's black youth. Its active alumni association includes a number of prominent citizens who might not have reached their potential had Loudoun County's black citizens not sacrificed and worked so hard to make the school a reality. Although no longer a segregated high school, Douglass serves the county today as an alternative school, meeting the special needs of students with various problems.

253-70

CHARLES RICHARD DREW HOUSE

2505 First Street S, Arlington County

Virginia Landmarks Register, February 15, 1977
National Historic Landmark, May 11, 1976

Charles Richard Drew, M.D. (1904–1950), was one of the pioneers of American medicine. This Afro-American physician's research and discoveries concerning blood plasma on the brink of World War II led to saving the lives of thousands of American soldiers. Since then, countless other people requiring transfusions have been similarly saved through the use of blood plasma.

Born in Washington, D.C., Drew was graduated from Amherst College and received the degree of Doctor of Medicine and Master of Surgery from McGill University in Montreal, where he concentrated in blood research. Returning to the Washington area, he became an instructor of pathology at Howard University. In

Dr. Charles Richard Drew

1938 Dr. Drew received a Rockefeller fellowship to study at Columbia University where he devoted much time to the study of the importance of blood plasma. Upon his graduation from Columbia in 1940, Dr. Drew became the first black in the nation to receive the Doctor of Science degree in surgery. At Columbia, Drew and his aides made the breakthrough conclusion that with proper preparation blood plasma could be safely stored almost indefinitely.

With the outbreak of World War II, the Blood for Britain Program was organized under the direction of Drew's former professor at McGill, Dr. John Beattie. Aware of Drew's medical and organizational skills, Dr. Beattie was instrumental in having him appointed director of the Blood for Britain section of the Blood Transfusion Association in New York. Dr. Drew immediately established uniform procedures for blood collection. In the expectation that the United States would enter the war, Drew was chosen to head the drive for plasma for use by American forces. As a result, Pearl Harbor did not catch American doctors unprepared. Because of Drew's efforts life-sustaining plasma was immediately available to the victims of Pearl Harbor and on the battlefields thereafter.

Unfortunately, Dr. Drew's work was thwarted in part by a newly established government policy requiring that blood from blacks and whites be segregated. Such an overtly racist policy forced Drew to resign his position, stating: "In the laboratory I have found that you and I share a common blood; but will we ever, ever share a common brotherhood?" (Aaron E. Klein, *The Hidden Contributors: Black Scientists and Inventors in America*). He then turned his attention to the education of black doctors and was active in the opening of white hospitals to black interns and residents. The armed forces eventually relaxed the policy of segregating blood, and in 1949 Drew accepted the appointment of surgical consultant to the surgeon general of the army. Drew's career was cut short when he was killed in an automobile accident in 1950. Senator Hubert Humphrey memorialized Dr. Drew on the floor of the U.S. Senate, stating that thousands owed their lives to his efforts.

The simple wooden house on First Street in Arlington was Dr. Drew's official residence between 1920 and 1939. The house was acquired as a relatively new structure by Drew's parents in 1920.

00-16

EXECUTIVE MANSION

Capitol Square, Richmond

Virginia Landmarks Register, November 5, 1968
National Register of Historic Places, June 4, 1969
National Historic Landmark, June 7, 1988

Virginia's Executive Mansion, also known as the Governor's Mansion, achieved a prominent place in the history of Afro-Americans in 1990 when it became the residence of Governor Lawrence Douglas Wilder, the first elected black governor in America since Reconstruction. A native of Richmond and grandson of slaves, Governor Wilder also served as Virginia's first black lieutenant governor.

In 1993 the body of tennis champion Arthur Ashe lay in state in the mansion, at the request of Governor Wilder, as thousands of mourners filed by. It was the first such ceremony since 1863, when the same honor was accorded the body of General

Thomas J. ("Stonewall") Jackson. Ashe, also a Richmond native, achieved fame as the first black to win the United States Tennis Open and the Wimbledon Men's Singles Championship.

Other occupants of the mansion have also played a role in black history. On the night of August 21–22, 1831, during the administration of Governor John Floyd, Nat Turner, a slave preacher, began an insurrection in Southampton County. Turner and his men killed about sixty whites. After two days militiamen and armed civilians quelled the revolt. Turner was captured on October 30, tried and convicted, and hanged on November 11; some thirty blacks were hanged or expelled from Virginia during the hysteria that followed the uprising. When the General Assembly convened in December 1831, Governor Floyd wrote in his diary that the "question of the gradual abolition of slavery . . . must come if I can influence my friends in the Assembly to bring it on. I will not rest until slavery is abolished in Virginia" (Charles H. Ambler, *The Life and Diary of John Floyd)*. Despite Floyd's efforts, however, the legislature passed harsher slave laws and censored abolitionist literature. It was the last serious public consideration of the abolition of slavery in the South before the Civil War.

After the war James Lawson Kemper, a former Confederate general, served as governor between 1874 and 1878. Although he campaigned as a conservative, once Kemper took office, to the surprise of many he proved himself an independent and pragmatic politician. In race relations, for instance, Kemper "sought to demonstrate to the North and the federal government that Virginia recognized the equality of the races before the law and would defend the rights of black Virginians" (Edward Younger and James Tice Moore, eds., *The Governors of Virginia, 1860–1978)*. Kemper also tried unsuccessfully to put the new, fragile public school system—which greatly benefited black children—on a better financial and legal footing.

Designed by architect Alexander Parris and competed in 1813, the elegant Federal structure is the oldest governor's mansion built as such in the United States.

127-57

Lawrence Douglas Wilder, governor of Virginia, 1990–94

FIRST BAPTIST CHURCH

418 Bute Street, Norfolk

Virginia Landmarks Register, April 19, 1983
National Register of Historic Places, July 21, 1983

One of the grandest architectural landmarks of downtown Norfolk, the First Baptist Church is a monument to the economic strength of Norfolk's blacks at the turn of the century and reflects the importance of religious institutions in the life of black Americans. The church is also an outstanding example of the Romanesque Revival, an architectural style which became popular throughout America beginning in the 1880s. It was designed by Chattanooga architect Reuben H. Hunt, a master of the style, and completed in 1906.

Regarded as the mother church of Norfolk's black Baptists, First Baptist's congregation was organized in 1800 and originally consisted of whites, free Negroes, and slaves. In 1805 the growing congregation occupied the Borough Church, Norfolk's colonial Anglican church (known today as St. Paul's Church), which had been abandoned with the disestablishment. In 1816 a group of the white members of the congregation grew dissatisfied with the large number of blacks in their midst and left to form the Cumberland Baptist Church. Although the congregation remained an integrated community and was led by a white pastor, First Baptist thenceforth was regarded as a "colored" congregation.

The present Bute Street site was acquired in 1830, and on it was erected a small wooden church known as the Old Salt Box. This in turn was replaced in 1877 by a brick church which served the congregation until it was demolished in 1904 to make way for the present building. The new church was an ambitious undertaking but was consistent with the growing prosperity of Norfolk's black community. By the end of the nineteenth century, Norfolk's blacks had obtained one of the highest levels of personal wealth and property ownership by blacks in the state. Much of this affluence reflected the city's growth as a transportation and shipping center, providing attractive salaries for the local labor force.

When it was opened in 1906, the new First Baptist, with its massive Romanesque facade and tower faced in pink New England granite, was praised by the local press as the handsomest church owned by the race in the south" (*Virginian Pilot,* May 6, 1906). At the dedication ceremony Norfolk's mayor called First Baptist "a monument to the race which would be handed down from a race that loved

First Baptist Church, Norfolk

God" (*Richmond Planet,* May 12, 1906). Much of the actual construction was done by members of the church; bake sales were held to raise funds to purchase bricks and offset the $52,000 cost of the project. Leadership for the effort was provided by the pastor, Richard H. Bowling. The resulting edifice is regarded as one of the most important works of the architect, Reuben H. Hunt, who designed prominent ecclesiastical buildings throughout the South, including the stylistically similar Court Street Baptist Church in Portsmouth.

122-40

The Old Salt Box Church

FIRST BAPTIST CHURCH
407 North Jefferson Street, NW, Roanoke

Virginia Landmarks Register, August 21, 1990
National Register of Historic Places, December 6, 1990

Roanoke's First Baptist Church was built in 1898–1900 to house what was at the time the largest and most prominent black congregation in Virginia west of Richmond. Designed by the ambitious local white architect H. H. Huggins, the church

The Reverend Richard R. Jones

is an imposing, if freely interpreted, essay in late Victorian Gothic, its simple but solid lines being appropriate to the simple liturgy of black Baptist worship. Like many urban black churches, First Baptist during its early years played a vital role in the lives of the city's black citizens and ultimately encouraged its leading members to become active in the affairs of the community at large. The church brought to its congregation, composed at the turn of the century largely of railroad workers, both spiritual nourishment and social stability.

The origins of the congregation date to 1855 when Dr. Charles L. Cocke, president of Hollins Institute (now Hollins College), established a Bible class for slaves in Big Lick. Dr. Cocke's Bible class soon grew into a full congregation and began meeting in 1867 in an old dwelling on Hart Avenue. By 1876 the congregation was able to purchase the old St. John's Episcopal Church for its new home.

The arrival of the Norfolk and Western Railroad in 1882 in Big Lick, incorporated that same year as the city of Roanoke, brought with it a large influx of workers, both black and white. This rapid population growth expanded the congregation of First Baptist over the next decade to the point that a much larger house of worship was required. Under the leadership of the Reverend Richard R. Jones, the church was able to secure a site near the railroad yards and build an impressive new edifice. Reporting on the upcoming dedication services of May 6, 1900, the local newspaper stated: "The new church is a handsome building and has been completed after a long and hard struggle on the part of the First church members. It is most creditable in every respect and immediately impresses the visitor as being the handsomest colored church in the city" (*Roanoke Times*, May 1, 1900).

First Baptist enjoyed a particularly active period during the long pastorate of the Reverend Arthur L. James from 1919 to 1958. During those years the church established a vacation Bible school ministering to over two hundred children each summer. Men's and women's organizations were formed to assist the poor. The Men's Club began publication of the *Church News*, reportedly the only black newspaper in southwest Virginia at the time. In 1930 Reverend James began the church's pioneering weekly radio broadcast, the "Back Home Devotional Hour." Membership peaked in the 1930s at more than two thousand, making First Baptist the largest black church in the western half of the state.

In 1982 the congregation left its Jefferson Street building for a new church a block away. Plans are currently underway to convert the landmark Gothic building into a performing arts center.

128-37

First Baptist Church interior

FIRST CALVARY BAPTIST CHURCH

1036-1040 Wide Street, Norfolk

Virginia Landmarks Register, June 17, 1987
National Register of Historic Places, October 15, 1987

The religious zeal of Norfolk's rapidly growing black community at the turn of this century was manifested in the prodigious churches erected by the various denominations. Conspicuous among them is First Calvary Baptist Church, a monumental

Georgian Revival edifice of red brick with a lavish display of white terra-cotta ornamentation. Dedicated in 1916, the church was designed by Mitchell & Wilcox, one of Norfolk's leading architectural firms. With its Corinthian columns, balustrades, finials, and wedding-cake belfry, the church has long been the principal landmark of Norfolk's Huntersville neighborhood. It is also one of the state's few black churches to have a distinctly eighteenth-century English architectural character.

Norfolk's black population grew significantly in the early decades of the twentieth century. Much of the increase was caused by the migration of blacks from the countryside to the city during World War I. Because the church was at the heart of black community life, new and larger church buildings were required to serve the religious needs of the expanding population. Organized in 1880 with only four members, First Calvary Baptist Church saw its congregation grow to more than fifteen hundred over the following four decades. Under the leadership of Dr. Percy J. Wallace, pastor from 1908 to 1922, First Calvary became one of the most influential black churches in the country. The need for a larger facility became evident, and Dr. Wallace was instrumental in getting the present church built.

Dr. Percy J. Wallace

The new building was completed at a cost of $90,000, a large sum at the time. Remarkably, the members paid off the debt in only two years, a significant accomplishment for a congregation made up not of wealthy individuals but of people who held a variety of low-income positions such as maids, cooks, butlers, laundry workers, small shopkeepers, and naval base employees.

The new church had a powerful impact. One member recalled the day of dedication: "He (Reverend Wallace) lined us all up, two-by-two, and we marched from Church Street to Wide and Henry.... And when we reached our new church, Glory be!" ("First Calvary Baptist Church," MS in VDHR Archives). The fervor that helped get the church erected was evident in the activities it housed. In the early years some members spent all day Sunday attending services, from the early meeting through Sunday School, the 11:30 service, the 3:00 P.M. service, 5:00 P.M. youth programs, and a night service. With an extensive educational building erected in 1968 and a renovation of the church interior in 1979, First Calvary, under the leadership of Dr. J. L. White, Sr., continues as a forceful institution for Norfolk's black Baptists.

122-73

Groundbreaking ceremonies for First Calvary Educational Building, 1949

FORT MONROE

Old Point Comfort, Hampton

Virginia Landmarks Register, September 9, 1969
National Historic Landmark, December 19, 1960

An outstanding example of an early nineteenth-century fortification, Fort Monroe was built between 1819 and 1834 at Old Point Comfort, a point of land at the entrance of Hampton Roads. The fort is probably best known for its moat, sturdy masonry walls, and impressive collection of military structures. With its commanding view of Hampton Roads and the Chesapeake Bay, Fort Monroe served as an important element of coastal defense, especially during the Civil War, when it became noted as a haven for slaves.

Freedmen at Fort Monroe, circa 1870

In 1861 Fort Monroe was garrisoned with a small force of U.S. Army soldiers which soon was reinforced. It became the headquarters of the Union Department of Virginia, which subsequently was combined with the Department of Virginia and North Carolina. The fort's association with Afro-American history emerged when its commander, Major General Benjamin F. Butler, decided to accept escaping slaves as "contrabands of war."

Before Butler made his innovative decision, fleeing slaves had been returned to the owners who claimed them. When a group of slaves who had been laboring on Confederate defensive works nearby escaped to the fort, however, Butler ordered them classed as war materiel—"contrabands"—and refused to surrender them. Word spread quickly, and thousands of slaves descended on the area. Fort Monroe became known to them as the Freedom Fort. The First and Second Regiments of U.S. Colored and Battery B, Second U.S. Colored Light Artillery, were raised there during the war. In 1865 the Bureau for the Relief of Freemen and Refugees ("Freedmen's Bureau") established its state headquarters at Fort Monroe.

As the slaves fled to the fort, the black population of Hampton and the surrounding area swelled, and the society that developed had a marked effect on the community. The need to have the former slaves achieve self-reliance and thus become productive members of the community led to the founding of Hampton Normal and Agricultural Institute (now Hampton University), a short distance from the fort. The school grew quickly into one of the nation's most important institutions of higher learning for blacks.

The Hampton area's newly acquired black population, which soon outnumbered the whites, settled mainly in the area immediately adjacent to the fort. The area was incorporated as the town of Phoebus in 1900 and was later annexed by Hampton. Phoebus blacks made up much of the fort's labor force. Phoebus also became a place of opportunity for newly emerging black entrepreneurs.

Fort Monroe was a symbol of freedom for blacks, but for former Confederate president Jefferson Davis it was just the opposite. Following his capture by Union authorities, Davis was held prisoner in one of the fort's casemates from 1865 to 1867.

114-2

FOURTH BAPTIST CHURCH

2800 P Street, Richmond

Virginia Landmarks Register, May 15, 1979
National Register of Historic Places, September 7, 1979

Fourth Baptist Church, the first black Baptist church in the Church Hill community in Richmond, is a symbol of the black religious strength in the Confederacy's
former capital during the decades following emancipation. Throughout the antebellum period most of Richmond's slave owners allowed their slaves the freedom
to worship on Sundays, most commonly in their own quarters. As with a number

Fourth Baptist Church interior

of black churches, the Fourth Baptist congregation began before 1861 as a regular assembly of slaves for prayer. The group, which grew in numbers, met regularly on Chimborazo Hill until the outbreak of the Civil War, when the white congregation of the Leigh Street Baptist Church granted permission for the slaves to hold their services in the church basement.

In 1865 the Reverend Scott Gwathmey, one of the prayer leaders, gained permission for the group to meet in a Union barracks on Chimborazo Hill. There, on December 2, 1965, the Fourth Baptist Church was formally organized, with Reverend Gwathmey serving as the first pastor. When eventually the barracks were demolished, the congregation salvaged lumber from the debris and constructed their own church building. In 1875 this church was replaced by another one of frame, on the northern side of Church Hill, near what was to be the site of the present church. The present building was completed in 1884, three months after the former church was destroyed by fire.

The dignified Greek Revival edifice, with its handsomely appointed interior, shows well how far the congregation had come in just two decades: from slave quarters to a basement and then a barracks, and finally to one of the city's more handsome houses of worship. The design of the church, with its Doric portico *in muris,* was inspired by the mother church of Richmond's Baptists, the First Baptist Church, designed by Thomas U. Walter of Philadelphia. Walter's well-known building, completed in 1841, was the architectural prototype of several Richmond Baptist churches, including the First African Baptist Church of 1876. The use of the Greek Revival temple form by Fourth Baptist more than forty years after it was introduced in Richmond illustrates both the sustained popularity of Walter's design and the architectural conservatism of Richmond's blacks in the late nineteenth century. The church continues to house one of Richmond's oldest black congregations.

127-318

FRANKLIN AND ARMFIELD OFFICE

1315 Duke Street, Alexandria

Virginia Landmarks Register, October 16, 1979
National Historic Landmark, June 2, 1978

This unprepossessing Alexandria town house is a relic of what was probably the most deplorable aspect of black life in the nation's history. From this structure the firm of Franklin and Armfield, the largest slave-trading operation in the antebellum South, was managed. The firm had its origins in 1824 when Isaac Franklin, a New Orleans slave dealer, befriended John Armfield, a North Carolina stagecoach driver and Franklin's nephew by marriage, and taught him his dubious trade. They formed a partnership in 1828 and established their headquarters on Duke Street in Alexandria. The city was craftily chosen because the area had a surplus of slaves available at low prices.

Franklin and Armfield Office, circa 1865

Armfield remained at 1315 Duke Street while Franklin set up sales offices in New Orleans and Natchez where slaves brought the highest prices. Using newspaper advertisements and a series of agents scouring the countryside, Armfield secured for his partner a steady supply of human chattel. Typical of the firm's many advertisements is one stating: "We will give Cash for one hundred likely YOUNG NEGROES of both sexes, between the ages of 8 and 25 years. Persons who wish to sell, would do well to give us a call, as the negroes are wanted immediately. We will give more than any other purchasers that are in the market or may hereafter come into the market" (*Alexandria Phenix Gazette,* December 12, 1828). The newly acquired slaves were held at Duke Street—which also served as Armfield's residence—until they could be transported south. At night they slept in the two-story rear wing where the doors and windows were grated like jails. During the day they were kept in a series of partially roofed courts or pens behind the property's high brick wall. At the peak of its success in the 1830s, the Franklin and Armfield firm was transporting from Alexandria to New Orleans one thousand to twelve hundred slaves annually. Most were carried in the firm's own ships, which sailed every thirty days during the shipping season from October to May.

Franklin and Armfield Office slave cells, circa 1865

Franklin and Armfield ran their business skillfully and efficiently; each partner amassed a considerable fortune. Franklin removed himself from active involvement with the trade in 1836, and the firm thereupon closed its Alexandria office. The Duke Street property was sold in 1846 to George Kephart, another slave dealer. In 1858 Kephart sold the establishment to Price, Birch, and Company, which continued a slave trade there until 1861 when the property was sold to Solomon Stover, ten days after Alexandria came under Union occupation. Ironically, during the Civil War, Union forces used the property to imprison captured Confederate soldiers. In 1870 the house, originally built about 1812 for Robert Young, a brigadier general in the District of Columbia militia, was purchased by Thomas Swann, a railroad builder. Swann tore down the slave pens and constructed a row of houses on their site. He also added a fourth story to the original house and altered the window openings. From 1878 to 1885 the building served as the Alexandria hospital. The property was renovated in recent years for office use. Little tangible evidence remains of the misery suffered by the thousands of black slaves who passed through the place over a thirty-three-year period.

100-105

FRYING PAN MEETINGHOUSE

2615 Centreville Road, Floris, Fairfax County

Virginia Landmarks Register, December 11, 1990
National Register of Historic Places, February 5, 1991

During the eighteenth and early nineteenth centuries, the Baptists were among the few religious groups in Virginia that were openly accepting of blacks, being essentially oblivious to racial differences. Frying Pan Meetinghouse is one of the oldest surviving Baptist churches in the state where a racially integrated congregation was maintained from the very beginning. The church traces its origins to 1775 when a Baptist congregation was organized at nearly Bull Run and chose Elder Richard Major as its pastor. Some of its members later wrote to Robert ("Councillor") Carter requesting his permission to build a meetinghouse on two acres of land he owned near Frying Pan Spring. Carter agreed, and the present structure, erected by members of the congregation, was standing by 1791. The wood-frame meetinghouse, little altered since its completion, is in the plain vernacular style favored by nonconformists. Elder Richard Major served as the first pastor of Frying Pan and was succeeded in 1797 by Elder Jeremiah Moore, who achieved fame before the Revolution by challenging the law that decreed that preachers must be licensed.

From the time of its completion, free blacks as well as slaves were welcomed as members of the Frying Pan congregation. Blacks spoke freely of their religious experiences in congregational meetings and were baptized along with whites in nearby Frying Pan Run. The congregation, however, maintained separate seating

Sunday morning, circa 1910, Frying Pan Meetinghouse

between blacks and whites, and blacks had a separate entrance. While both blacks and whites were buried in the church cemetery, a custom observed almost exclusively by Baptists, blacks were placed in a separate area. By 1840 Frying Pan had twenty-nine black members and thirty-three white members. Following the Civil War it became legally permissible for blacks in Virginia to have their own churches with black preachers. Thus after 1867 blacks in the area organized a black Baptist congregation and in 1882 constructed Mount Pleasant Baptist Church not far away.

In 1984 Arthur L. Carter, the last surviving trustee of the congregation, deeded the meetinghouse property to the Fairfax County Park Authority. As funds become available, the meetinghouse and adjacent sites, including the cemetery and Frying Pan Spring—which provided fresh water for both the members and their horses—will be developed as a museum interpreting the early religious life of the area's Baptists. The role of Fairfax County's early blacks will be an important component of this story.

Frying Pan Meetinghouse derives its unusual name from a local legend which holds that some Indians camped on the run and left behind their frying pan containing their meal when attacked by two white settlers. The name "Frying Pan" appears on local maps as early as 1725.

29-15

Virginia-Cleveland Hall, Hampton University

HAMPTON INSTITUTE (HAMPTON UNIVERSITY)

East Queen Street, Hampton

Virginia Landmarks Register, September 9, 1969
National Register of Historic Places, November 12, 1969
National Historic Landmark, May 30, 1974

Hampton Institute is among the nation's most noted landmarks of our Afro-American heritage, a symbol of one of the first and most important efforts to bring blacks into the mainstream of American life. Brevet Brigadier General Samuel Chapman Armstrong (1839–1893), then chief of the local Freedmen's Bu-

General Samuel Chapman Armstrong

reau, founded the school in 1868 to serve the growing community of freed people who had gathered in the Hampton area during and immediately after the Civil War. Through Armstrong's urging the American Missionary Association purchased a 165-acre farm where the federal government had maintained a hospital during the war. Armstrong's vision was to use the property to train selected young black and Indian men and women "who should go out and teach and lead their people, first by example ... and in this way build up an industrial system for the sake, not only of self-support and intelligent labor, but also for the sake of character" (Francis G. Peabody, *Education for Life: The Story of Hampton Institute)*. The school opened with only two teachers and fifteen pupils, with Armstrong as principal.

Armstrong modeled Hampton after the Hilo Manual Labor School in Hawaii where his father had served as Hawaiian minister of education. Armstrong's philosophy, which emphasized training of "the head, the hand, and the heart," placed priority on preparing teachers and acquiring the Puritan work ethic and moral values. The school prospered under Armstrong's leadership, and by 1870 it was chartered as the Hampton Normal and Agricultural Institute.

Classes at Hampton were originally held in makeshift quarters in the old hospital barracks. The institute's leaders, however, had ambitious plans. By 1874 the imposing Virginia-Cleveland Hall was completed after the designs of the noted architect Richard Morris Hunt, with construction carried out in part by the students. Hunt also designed the Academic Hall, completed in 1881. It is ironic that Hunt, who devoted his career chiefly to designing enormous mansions for American millionaires, was also the architect for buildings to serve recently freed people. The historic core of the campus also includes a distinctive Romanesque Revival chapel designed by J. C. Cady and completed in 1886.

Hampton's most famous graduate was Booker T. Washington of the class of 1875, who adopted Armstrong's self-help ideology and applied it at Tuskegee Institute, which he founded in 1881. Now known as Hampton University, Armstrong's school has grown into a modern institution with more than five thousand under-

Hampton Institute classroom, 1907

graduate and graduate students and some 150 buildings. Though its enrollment is predominantly Afro-American, Hampton is a racially integrated, nonsectarian institution. Still alive on the campus is the Emancipation Oak, under whose massive boughs the Emancipation Proclamation was read in 1863 to the Hampton residents. Legend has it that here were taught the first classes of the institution.

114-06

HARRISON SCHOOL

523 Harrison Street, NW, Roanoke

Virginia Landmarks Register, May 18, 1982
National Register of Historic Places, September 9, 1982

Completed in 1917, Roanoke's Harrison School marks a milestone in the history of black secondary education in southwest Virginia. By 1915 only 1,761 black pupils were enrolled in Virginia high schools, compared to 23, 184 white pupils. The prevailing educational theory at the time was that blacks should receive industrial rather than academic instruction beyond the seventh grade.

Roanoke-area blacks who wanted more than an elementary education had to travel nearly two hundred miles to Virginia State College in Petersburg. This dis-

Lucy Addison

couraging situation was rectified by Miss Lucy Addison (1861–1937), the first principal of Harrison School and a strong advocate of academic education for members of her race. Harrison School, the fourth black public school in Roanoke, was
originally intended only for primary education. Miss Addison, a native of Fauquier
County educated in the public schools of Philadelphia and at Howard University,
was responsible for gradually extending the curriculum of Harrison School beyond the primary level by adding a half year of high school classes each calendar
year. The first class to complete four full years of high school under her tutelage
graduated in 1924. The growing demand for high school education for Roanoke's
blacks resulted in the construction of a new high school in 1928, appropriately
named for Miss Addison.

Harrison School, although not as architecturally ambitious as the city's white schools, was a thoroughly modern and commodious facility for its time, costing $31,818. Its design reflected the Georgian style, a style popular at the time for public buildings, especially schools. Plans for the building were drawn by J. H. Page, clerk of the school board; the contractor was J. F. Barbour. As with many black public schools during the era of segregation, Harrison School became a focal point for black cultural enrichment programs and social activities. Its students were visited by Booker T. Washington, George Washington Carver, and Jesse Owens, as well as by various black entertainers.

Harrison School closed with the end of segregated schools in the 1960s. The building was used for a time as a day care center and then stood vacant until 1983 when title was transferred by the city to the Harrison School Limited Partnership, which undertook a certified rehabilitation of the structure for housing for the elderly. A model of adaptive reuse, the new facility opened in December 1985. Included in the building is the Harrison Museum of African American Culture, a museum focusing on the history of the black community of the Roanoke Valley.

128-43

HOLLEY GRADED SCHOOL

Lottsburg, Northumberland County

Virginia Landmarks Register, April 18, 1989
National Register of Historic Places, December 19, 1990

The Holley Graded School represents the dedicated work of many members of a
small black community on the Northern Neck who, despite economic hardship
and the deterrence of segregation, erected a schoolhouse which was remarkably
large and well appointed both for its time and the people it served. For nearly forty
years the school helped open the doors to the larger world and greater opportunities for rural black children. It also provided hope, support, and social cohesion
during an era of institutionalized racial discrimination.

The present school was begun circa 1914 to replace a smaller schoolhouse erected during the Reconstruction era. It stands on two acres purchased shortly after
the Civil War by Sallie Holley (1818–1893), a native of New York State, for whom

Sallie Holley

the school was later named. An ardent abolitionist and advocate of universal suff-
rage, Holley followed the example of her friend Emily Howland and established a
school for children of former slaves in Northumberland County in 1869. Holley's
one-room school was a relatively insubstantial structure and was twice rebuilt. By
the 1910s the third structure had itself become dilapidated, and the local blacks ral-
lied to plan and construct with their own hands a new four-classroom structure.
Work on the new school progressed very slowly, only as funds became available.
The fourth and final classroom was not completed until 1933.

Built at a time when many white elementary schools were commodious modern facilities with indoor plumbing, central heating, libraries, and well-equipped
recreational areas, the Holley Graded School was primitive by comparison, with

woodstoves, outdoor privies, and nothing at all resembling swings, slides, or jungle gyms. There was, however, considerable local pride in the new school because it was achieved entirely through local effort. All construction funds were raised privately; no public funds, state or local, were used. Also, ownership and control of the school from 1917 on was vested in a board of trustees composed entirely of local blacks. While relatively modest in size, the Holley Graded School was the largest black school in the county when finally completed. Pride in the building was expressed by the fancy shingle work in the gable and the unusually elaborate stamped sheet metal used to decorate the walls and ceilings of the interior. Separate classrooms also represented a considerable advancement over the one-room structures standard for rural black students.

Holley School served the community until 1959 when a new consolidated school for blacks opened in Lottsburg. The building stood unoccupied until the mid-1960s when it began being used by locals for playing pool. Through the efforts of Mrs. Ruth Blackwell, funds were raised to keep the building in repair. In the early 1980s, with Mrs. Blackwell's encouragement, the trustees developed plans to restore the school for use as a museum and community center. The building now houses the Adult Literacy Program of Northumberland County.

66-112

HOLLY KNOLL

Capahosic, Gloucester County

Virginia Landmarks Register, March 16, 1982
National Historic Landmark, December 21, 1981

Holly Knoll, on the banks of the York River, was the retirement home of the remarkably active and influential black educator Robert Russa Moton (1867–1940),
successor to Booker T. Washington at Tuskegee Institute. Moton was one of the
founders of the National Urban League and developed Tuskegee Institute from a

vocational and agricultural school to a fully accredited collegiate and professional institution. An adviser to five U.S. presidents, from Woodrow Wilson to Franklin D. Roosevelt, Moton sponsored Tuskegee's early studies in communicable diseases that eventually contributed to the passage of the Communicable Disease Act of 1938 and the establishment of the National Communicable Disease centers. Moton was also the author of three books dealing with black studies and race relations: *What the Negro Thinks, Racial Goodwill,* and *Finding a Way Out.*

Moton was born in Amelia County, Virginia, and spent his childhood years on the plantation of Samuel Vaughan in Prince Edward County, where his father "led the hands" and his mother was the cook. Vaughan had his daughter instruct young Moton in reading and encouraged his education. In 1885, at age eighteen, Moton

Robert Russa Moton

enrolled at Hampton Institute (present-day Hampton University). Upon graduation in 1890 he became the commandant in charge of military discipline at the institute, a post he held for twenty-five years. While in that position, he served as
Hampton's principal representative in the educational and interracial conferences,
commissions, and organizations fostered by the institute.

In 1915 Moton was chosen to succeed Booker T. Washington as principal at
Tuskegee Institute. During World War I he was successful in having Tuskegee establish a camp for the training of black officers. He also persuaded the secretary of
war to form a black combat division and to approve the appointment of Emmett
Scott, a black, as assistant secretary of war. Moton later was sent to France by President Wilson to inspect black troops and report on their morale. After the war he
succeeded in having black professional and service personnel assigned to the staff
of a federal hospital for black veterans near Tuskegee. On May 30, 1922, Moton de-
livered the main address at the dedication of the Lincoln Memorial in Washington, D.C.

Declining health forced Moton's retirement in 1935 as head of Tuskegee Institute after serving it for twenty years. That same year he built the large Georgian
Revival house in Gloucester County, Virginia, for his retirement, and he lived there
until his death in 1940. Moton also built on the property a replica of the lob cabin
in which he was born. Moton's columned mansion is now the core building of the
Robert R. Moton Memorial Institute, Inc., an organization perpetuating Moton's
ideals through operating a college endowment funding program and maintaining
the estate as an executive conference center.

36-134

Howard's Neck slave quarters

HOWARD'S NECK

Pemberton, Goochland County

Virginia Landmarks Register, November 16, 1971
National Register of Historic Places, February 23, 1972

The requirements for a slave-worked agricultural complex in antebellum Virginia is well illustrated in the diversity of buildings surviving at the upper James River plantation Howard's Neck. The centerpiece of the plantation is an architecturally refined Federal mansion built around 1825 for Edward Cunningham, a leader in the Richmond milling industry. Scattered about the mansion is a full complement of outbuildings including a kitchen, smokehouse, toolhouse, and orangery, buildings originally tended by slave servants.

The chief object of interest at Howard's Neck relating to slave life is a street of three slave quarters. This grouping is an exceptionally rare survival for nearly all such streets have vanished in Virginia. A study of the quarters undertaken by the Colonial Williamsburg Foundation suggests that these units were meant to house slaves tending the plantation's home quarter, that part of the plantation which included the main residence and its outbuildings. Large plantations such as Howard's Neck normally had more than one complex of slave quarters: the home quarters and the distant quarters. The distant quarters usually were very rude structures occupied by field hands, the lowest level of the slave social strata. The site of any distant quarters at Howard's Neck has not been found.

The three-building home quarters complex is located down the hill but out of sight from the main house. The remains of the foundations of a fourth unit are evident. A plat of the grounds prepared in 1930 suggests that a total of five quarters were standing at that time. Archaeological investigation would be necessary to determine the full extent of the complex. As with many such groups, an overseer's house is immediately adjacent. In this case the overseer's house is an early nineteenth-century story-and-a-half, frame structure with shed dormers and is situated farther down the hill facing the quarters. Each of the remaining quarters is a two-unit structure with a central brick chimney. This configuration was a standard one for nineteenth-century quarters because it could house two families while requiring only one chimney. The use of brick chimneys, as opposed to wood and mud chimneys, indicates that these were more substantial slave houses than usual. Each dwelling is also fronted by what is probably an original shed porch. Although all three structures are weatherboarded, the center house is of log construction while the outer two are of frame.

The quarters were upgraded in the late nineteenth century, probably as farm laborers' dwellings. The outer two houses were raised to two full stories; all three originally had just a loft upper level which was reached by a ladder stair. The lean-to additions on each unit likely were part of the upgrading, as was the installation of glazed sash windows. All the windows probably were initially served by sliding board shutters, one of which is intact in the center unit. The interior of the center house is probably closest to its original condition, having exposed log walls and ceiling joists and a board ceiling. The houses have not been occupied for many years and are currently being used for storage.

37-100

HOWLAND CHAPEL SCHOOL

Howland, Northumberland County

Virginia Landmarks Register, June 20, 1989
National Register of Historic Places, January 25, 1991

Howland Chapel School is a poignant reminder of the various efforts of idealistic
northerners to assist the children of Virginia's former slaves in the years following
the Civil War. The one-story frame building was erected under the sponsorship of
New York educator, reformer, and philanthropist Emily Howland (1827–1929), after whom it was named. It is also the oldest standing schoolhouse in Northumber-

land County and possibly the earliest public schoolhouse on the Northern Neck. Erected by local carpenters and laborers, Howland Chapel School for its time and place was unusually large and well built; most of Virginia's Reconstruction-era rural schools, black and white, were cramped, cheaply built structures that seldom lasted more than a decade or two. Howland School served continuously from 1867 to 1958. Until 1929, the year in which the Northumberland County school board assumed control of the property, Howland School was supported and maintained by Miss Howland and members of the local black community.

Emily Howland was born into a wealthy New York State Quaker family. Her father, Slocum Howland, was an abolitionist whose home in Scipio, New York,

Emily Howland

served occasionally as a station on the Underground Railroad. Miss Howland shared her father's sympathy for blacks and at age thirty-one began teaching in Miss Myrtilla Miner's school for free Negro girls in Washington, D.C. After the war Howland became increasingly frustrated with the government's failure to provide adequate support for freedmen. She thus devised a plan whereby she would assist former slaves herself by purchasing a tract of land and letting several black families settle there as independent farmers. Her acquaintance with freedmen from Northumberland County led her to carry out her plan there, beginning in 1866 with the purchase of a farm near Heathsville.

Soon after her arrival in Northumberland County, Howland began teaching in a small log cabin on her farm. The response to her efforts was encouraging: an average of forty children attended each day, and an equal number of adults came in the evenings. The cabin soon proved inadequate, and Howland and her neighbor Alexander Day, a free black, began planning a new schoolhouse which could also serve as a church. The building was completed in 1867, and Day insisted that it be named in her honor, calling it originally the Howland Chapel.

Miss Howland returned to the North in 1870, but for the next fifty years she continued to choose the school's teachers and pay their salaries as well as to bear the maintenance expenses. In 1986 the First Baptist Church of Heathsville acquired title to the school and began raising funds for its restoration. The church trustees plan to use the restored schoolhouse as a museum, community center, and adult-education facility.

66-110

Clay Street

JACKSON WARD HISTORIC DISTRICT
Richmond

Virginia Landmarks Register, April 20, 1976
National Register of Historic Places, July 30, 1976
National Historic Landmark, June 2, 1978

Richmond at the turn of this century had one of the most thriving black business communities in the nation. The hub of this professional and entrepreneurial activity was the Jackson Ward neighborhood in the heart of the city. Its many fraternal organizations, cooperative banks, insurance companies, churches, and other commercial and social institutions were all founded and run by blacks, including bankers Maggie L. Walker and John Mitchell, ministers W. W. Browne and John Jasper, Common Council members John H. Adams, Jr., and S. W. Robinson, and attorney Giles B. Jackson, the first black admitted for practice before the state

Bill ("Bojangles") Robinson

supreme court. The neighborhood's most popularly known son, however, was the dancer and motion-picture actor Bill ("Bojangles") Robinson.

In the decades before the Civil War, Jackson Ward developed as a neighborhood populated largely by citizens of German and Jewish extraction. At the same time a growing number of free blacks began to settle in the area. This community of black property owners, journeymen, and laborers was known locally as Little Africa and became a significant economic and social force in the Reconstruction era. The relative affluence and civic-mindedness of Richmond's black citizens, largely nurtured in Jackson Ward, resulted in one of the country's most stable and conservative black communities. Urban redevelopment and expressway construction have since reduced its size, but the forty blocks or fractions of blocks remaining make Jackson Ward the nation's largest National Historic Landmark historic district associated primarily with black history and culture.

In Jackson Ward was the first black-organized bank to be chartered in the United States, the true Reformers Bank. This was followed by Maggie Walker's St. Luke Penny Savings Bank and other black financial institutions. Becoming as it did an incubator of black capitalism, Jackson Ward for a time was known as the Black Wall Street of America. The 1940 publication *The Negro in Virginia* described Jackson Ward's principal commercial artery, noting that "along one or more blocks of Second Street in Richmond . . . the 'crowd' may be found almost every evening. For a block or two everything is Negro; here is a little oasis—'our street.'"

Among the district's principal landmarks are the Maggie L. Walker residence, now administered as a museum by the National Park Service, and the 1932 home of the merchant Adolph Dill, now the Black History Museum and Cultural Center of Virginia. Noteworthy churches of Jackson Ward include the 1870s Ebenezer Baptist Church, the largest church in the neighborhood; the Third Street Bethel A.M.E. Church, erected in 1857; and the 1888 Sixth Mount Zion Church, the church of the nationally renowned black preacher John Jasper.

The neighborhood is dominated by three-bay, side-passage town houses in Greek Revival, Italianate, and Queen Anne styles. Many of the Italianate houses have locally manufactured cast-iron porches, the states' richest display of ornamental ironwork. Despite commercial expansion, poverty, and neglect, the surviving portions of Jackson Ward form a remarkably cohesive urban community which recently has become the focus of increasing rehabilitation activity.

127-237

Conjectural view of early seventeenth-century Jamestown

JAMESTOWN
NATIONAL HISTORIC SITE

Jamestown Island, James City County

Virginia Landmarks Register, October 18, 1983
National Historic Site, December 18, 1940

The black experience in English America began in August 1619 with the first recorded arrival of Africans in the infant Virginia colony. Little is known of the exact circumstances of the coming of these blacks or how they were treated once they arrived. The sole reference to the event comes from a 1619/20 letter written by John Rolfe, the pioneer in tobacco cultivation, which was later quoted by Captain John Smith in his history of the colony. In his letter Rolfe stated that "twenty and odd" Africans were brought to Virginia aboard a Dutch man-of-war whose crew had captured them from the Spanish (John Rolfe to Sir Edwin Sandys, 1619/20,

The Records of the Virginia Company of London). The Dutch apparently considered the blacks as booty since they exchanged them for provisions with the colony's governor, Sir George Yeardley, after they docked at Old Point Comfort. Yeardley in all likelihood first placed the blacks on his plantation at Jamestown, where he resided. Jamestown, in any case, has come to symbolize the genesis of Afro-American history.

How the English treated these first blacks has been the subject of much speculation. There is nothing to indicate that they were kept permanently as chattel. More likely they were treated as indentured servants who were later freed after their periods of servitude expired. On the other hand, there is no evidence that blacks were ever regarded as the social equals of the whites. Most Englishmen probably had no fixed attitudes about blacks since they had never before been forced to deal with them to any great extent. Interestingly, the earliest records that name blacks in Virginia, the musters of 1624 and 1625, show that many of them had Spanish names. If these records included the blacks who arrived in 1619, it would raise questions about their legal status, for had the blacks been baptized by the Spanish, they would have been free under existing English law, which forbade holding Christians against their will.

Whatever the status of America's first blacks, slavery, as it is perceived today, was not a fully established institution in Virginia until the 1660s, and many Africans were regarded as indentured servants during the intervening years. It took the formation of the great plantations toward the end of the seventeenth century to generate the need for a large agrarian labor force, one that could not be met in sufficient numbers by either the English or the Indians. The institution of slavery thus evolved as an economic necessity for the colony rather than springing full-blown into existence.

Although the lives of American blacks have been fraught with tribulation since 1619, this racial group has constituted an integral part of American civilization for nearly four centuries. From their first inauspicious and involuntary arrival on the banks of the James, blacks have become a distinctive and permanent part of the rich fabric of America. Their presence and their treatment ultimately has been the catalyst for forcing the nation to examine its soul and to face with conviction, as few other societies have, the age-old problems of injustice, racial prejudice, and political and social inequality.

47-09

The first documented Africans in English America arrived at Jamestown in August 1619. A Dutch man-of-war captured them from the Spanish, who had enslaved them, and sold them to the Virginia colonists. The "twenty and odd" Africans, some of whom had been given Spanish names, may have been treated like indentured servants and later freed after their periods of servitude expired. From this beginning the institution of slavery evolved during the 17th century as the Virginia colonists extended the length of service for Africans from a fixed term to life. The United States abolished slavery in 1865.

Governor L. Douglas Wilder unveiling the highway marker honoring the first Africans in English America

LITTLE ENGLAND CHAPEL
4100 Kecoughtan Road, Hampton

Virginia Landmarks Register, June 16, 1981
National Register of Historic Places, July 8, 1982

The diminutive Little England Chapel is a monument to the role of blacks in helping members of their own race achieve a better quality of life and a stronger sense of community through education and spiritual growth. During the Civil War southern blacks, in search of freedom, flocked to the Union-protected Hampton area. After the war many settled in the area known as Newtown, a tract of land made available to them by Daniel F. Cock, a New York missionary who came to Hampton as an instructor at nearby Hampton Institute (Hampton University). Cock purchased the property, in an area once known as Little England, to make it available for use by freedmen.

The forerunner of the Little England Chapel was the Ocean Cottage Sunday School established by George C. Rowe in 1877. Rowe, a religious man, had been hired as a printer at Hampton Institute and was residing across Hampton Creek from the institute. He began Sunday school classes with three Newtown children meeting in his home. The Sunday school became so popular that William Armstrong, brother of General Samuel Chapman Armstrong, founder of Hampton Institute, offered to erect a building, and Daniel Cock offered the use of land for a day school and Sunday School. General Armstrong contributed to funds raised by Newtown residents to support a teacher. The chapel was then constructed on Cock's land. Local legend attributes the construction to Hampton Institute students.

Completed in 1879 and originally called simply the "Sunday School" or the "Chapel," Little England Chapel in its first years served a variety of uses. Primarily the Hampton Institute students used it to provide Sunday school lessons to the Newtown youth. The students' visit was regarded as the high point of the week for the children. Black college students were then a novelty and held in great respect. The building also served as a community center for Newtown. In it were held programs of teaching and singing as well as concerts. The Newtown Improvement and Civic Club also held its meetings in the chapel and eventually assumed responsibility for upkeep. In 1886 Hampton Institute's records reported that the Sunday School had an attendance of seventy children and had engaged its young people in missionary work for the surrounding community. By 1890 the chapel

Little England Chapel

had become well known for its sewing school. The recollections of Emanuel R. Savage give a vivid image of chapel activities in its heyday: "I remember the Christmas parties, being served hot chocolate, preaching and praying of the men, being on the 'Mourners Bench,' the pealing of the bell, the teachers arriving in the shiny black 'Chariot' drawn by two large white horses, and especially, Mr. Johnson preaching and Mr. Glymph praying" ("Reflections," MS in VDHR Archives).

Hampton Institute students continued to teach at Little England Chapel into the mid-1930s. From 1939 to 1989 the building was used for worship services by the Church of Jesus. In 1954 Frederick D. Cock, son of Daniel F. Cock, deeded the chapel and its lot to the Newtown Improvement and Civic Club. The club incorporated in 1990 and undertook restoration of the building as a historical, community, and nondenominational religious center celebrating the area's Afro-American culture. A grand opening for the restored chapel was held May 23, 1993.

114-40

MADDEN'S TAVERN

Lignum Vicinity, Culpeper County

Virginia Landmarks Register, May 15, 1984
National Register of Historic Places, August 16, 1984

This simple log structure is one of the few relics of pre–Civil War black entrepreneurship surviving in rural Virginia. Completed about 1840, the tavern was built, owned, and operated by Willis Madden (1799–1879), a free black, and was likely the only tavern in the region with a proprietor of Madden's race. Madden was born to Sarah Madden, a mulatto, who at one time was bound out as an indentured servant to James Madison, Sr., of Orange County, father of the president. Because

Willis Madden

Sarah Madden was a free black woman, her children were also free under the law. Virginia free blacks were able to earn and keep wages and to own and operate businesses. Their lives were still very restricted as the laws forbade them to vote, bear arms, testify against a white person, or be taught to read and write. Taking advantage of his freedom, Willis Madden plied many trades to support his family including farm laborer, blacksmith, nailmaker, distiller, cobbler, and teamster.

In 1835 the ambitious Madden decided to go into the tavern business and purchased approximately eighty-seven acres in Culpeper County, near the junction of the Old Fredericksburg Road and the Peola Mills–Kellysville Road. There he erected the four-room core of the present structure, as well as several outbuildings. The western half of the tavern contained the family living quarters, and the eastern portion consisted of a downstairs public room and a loft for overnight guests. Madden never acquired a tavern license but operated under a loophole which exempted those who provided furnished camping facilities to teamsters and rovers. A general store and a blacksmith-wheelwright shop also stood on the property, offering employment for Madden's sons and relatives. The tavern was one of the best known in the county, and tavern records indicate that prominent local citizens, all white, were among its patrons.

The tavern business declined with the construction of the railroad in the 1850s. Extensive damage to the property committed by Union troops during the winter of 1863–64, including destruction of all the outbuildings, brought the business to an end. Since the Civil War the property has been used strictly for farming and residential purposes and has never left the Madden family. In 1949 T. O. Madden, Jr., Willis Madden's great-grandson, discovered in the attic a trunk containing family and tavern records, including Willis Madden's free papers. From these, he was able to document the family legends regarding his remarkable ancestor. Although enlarged and modernized Madden's Tavern is no longer the busy place it once was. It does retain, however, much of its original simple, rustic character.

23-29

MEADOW FARM

Glen Allen Vicinity, Henrico County

Virginia Landmarks Register, May 21, 1974
National Register of Historic Places, August 13, 1974

Meadow Farm, the Sheppard family plantation on the outskirts of Richmond, is the principal remaining site associated with the aborted slave insurrection conceived in 1800 by the slave Gabriel. Although the revolt was suppressed before any of Gabriel's ambitious and well-organized plans could be carried out, the very idea of the insurrection instilled a fear of blacks among Virginia's white citizenry. Blacks, both free and slave, became objects of suspicion and thenceforth were subjected to harsher laws designed to keep them under stricter control. The insurrection also foreshadowed the revolt of Nat Turner thirty years later which brought about even greater subjugation of the slaves.

On August 30, 1800, Tom and Pharaoh, Sheppard family slaves, entered Mosby Sheppard's office at Meadow Farm and told him the details of Gabriel's revolt, which was planned to take place that night. Gabriel, the slave of a neighboring planter, Thomas H. Prosser, believed he was ordained to deliver his people from bondage. Gabriel's intelligence, practical education, and knowledge of military science enabled him to develop a plan to raise a slave army of a thousand men to attack Richmond, seize the public arms, and kill all whites except the French, Quakers, and Methodists (to be spared because they believed in liberty) and non-slave-owning poor farmers. Once he captured Richmond, Gabriel planned to have himself crowned king of Virginia.

Sheppard immediately warned Governor James Monroe of the impending rebellion. Monroe placed guards at the capitol and where public weapons were stored and sent cavalry to protect the routes into Richmond. Slave conspirators were rounded up over the following week; by September 13 ten had been executed. Gabriel was eventually captured in Norfolk where he was trying to flee aboard a schooner. He was executed on October 7. By the end of the investigation, a total of forty-one slaves had been put to death for their part in the plot. Tom and Pharaoh, the two who had warned Sheppard of the plan, were purchased by the Commonwealth and given their freedom.

Although Virginia had experienced isolated slave revolts before, the scale and organization of Gabriel's planned revolt prompted a deep-seated fear of blacks throughout the state and indeed much of the South. In addition to the laws passed to place further restrictions on the movements of blacks, the city of Richmond instituted a public guard which for the next half century stood sentinel against similar threats. Gabriel's revolt also planted the seeds for the formation in 1816 of the American Colonization Society, which established the Negro colony of Liberia as a place to send free blacks and dangerous slaves, many of whom came from Virginia. The harsh reaction to Gabriel's insurrection caused many northerners to sympathize more overtly with the plight of the slaves, fueling the Abolitionist movement. Meadow Farm today is exhibited as a farm museum operated by Henrico County. The present house, begun in 1810, replaced the Sheppard house standing at the time of the insurrection.

43-31

MONTICELLO

Charlottesville Vicinity, Albemarle County

Virginia Landmarks Register, September 9, 1969
National Historic Landmark, December 19, 1960

Thomas Jefferson's mountaintop home Monticello, one of the most famous houses in America, is widely admired for its innovative architecture. Jefferson began his dwelling on the "Little Mountain" in 1770 and worked on it for more than forty years. While most people perceive his home chiefly as an elegant isolated dwelling, Monticello historically was actually an assemblage of buildings, structures, and outdoor spaces forming a major Virginia plantation complex, one requiring a large number of servants and other types of laborers to maintain. Jefferson, although an exceptional individual in many ways, was typical of most upper-class Virginia planters in being a slave owner. Monticello could not have existed without such a labor force.

At its peak more than fifty slaves were living and working on the mountaintop, tending the busy complex. This facet of Monticello was little appreciated until recently because most of the slave dwellings and associated structures, aligned along what was known as Mulberry Row, had disappeared. Of the service structures, only the working areas of the house itself—the kitchen, pantry, storerooms, and related work spaces, located in the long, partially subterranean wings extending from the mansion—remained.

Research into the role of blacks in the operation of this presidential seat began in the 1970s and was greatly expanded in 1979 with the excavations of Mulberry Row directed by archaeologist William Kelso. Over the following decade the excavations revealed the remains of more than a score of houses, light industrial buildings, and yards. Within these sites were found thousands of day-to-day artifacts of the slave community that provided remarkable insights into African-American material culture. Together, these remnants of a mountaintop labor force showed that in spite of the severely handicapping condition of slavery, Monticello's black community was as complex and vibrant as any other segment of early Virginia society.

The digging revealed that slaves lived in a variety of houses, from the smallest, rudest log cabin with earth floors and wooden chimneys to substantial stone buildings with masonry fireplaces and wooden floors. The Mulberry Row artifacts such as pottery, glass, and leisure-time objects indicate that the slaves were using

Mulberry Row excavations at Monticello

materials similar in quality to some used by the Jefferson family in the main house. While the slave artifacts are almost exclusively Anglo-American, some objects, such as primitive jewelry, show a surviving African spiritual tradition. Food rations for slaves, reflected in discarded animal bones, leave little doubt that certain individuals had a richer diet than Jefferson's records of the items he supplied them indicate. The Mulberry Row foundations and the many associated artifacts now are an important part of the museum interpretation at Monticello.

While slave life at Monticello was probably not much different from that on the plantations of other Virginia patricians, no other excavations in the Common-wealth have provided such a quantity of information on the subject. Jefferson, one of the greatest heroes of democracy, is frequently criticized for having owned slaves. But in this area, especially, he was a product of his time, enslaved to a system he could not afford to abandon.

02-50

Slave possessions excavated at Mulberry Row: pierced eighteenth-century Spanish coins, African cowrie shell, and horn ring

MOUNT VERNON

Alexandria Vicinity, Fairfax County

Virginia Landmarks Register, September 9, 1969
National Historic Landmark, December 19, 1960

If Mount Vernon is the great symbol of George Washington the husband, family man, and planter, it also stands as a reminder of his crisis of conscience, one which he confronted and resolved by eventually emancipating the black slaves who labored there. Many of the slaveholders who led the American Revolution were troubled by the distance between their ideals and reality, particularly with regard to the institution of slavery. How could men who fought for freedom and independence, and who would themselves choose death over what they regarded as political slavery, reconcile the lofty words of the Declaration of Independence with the continued servitude of black men and women? The question disturbed no leader more than Washington, under whose generalship the country gained its independence. To many Americans, Washington was the personification of nationhood, and he was a man well aware of his place in history.

Washington, like many of his contemporaries, harbored a hope from gradual emancipation. In 1797 he wrote, "I wish from my soul that the Legislature of this State could see the policy of a gradual abolition of slavery; it would prevent much future mischief" (Washington to Lawrence Lewis, Aug. 4, 1797 in Douglas Southall Freeman, *George Washington*). In the absence of action by an outside agency such

Washington as a Farmer at Mount Vernon, *1851, by Junius Brutus Stearns*

as the General Assembly, Washington was thrown on his own resources. He was "principled against selling Negroes, as you would cattle in the market," and likewise resolved "never again to become the master of another slave by purchase" (ibid.).

In theory, Washington could have emancipated his slaves by a stroke of his pen, but by doing so he would have destroyed his own fortune and that of his family. His situation was complicated by the fact that many of the slaves at Mount Vernon were in fact the dower property of his wife Martha, and he could not legally emancipate them. Furthermore, some of them had intermarried with Washington's own slaves. How could he free a slave father whom he owned and not emancipate the mother (Martha's property) and their child as well?

Washington compromised, freeing only one slave at his death, and all the others at Martha Washington's death. He explained that

upon the decease of my wife, it is my will and desire that all the slaves which I hold in my own right shall receive their freedom. To emancipate them during her life, would, though earnestly wished by me, be attended with such insuperable difficulties on account of their intermixture by marriage with the Dower Negroes, as to excite the most painful sensations, if not disagreeable consequences from the latter, while both descriptions are in the occupancy of the same proprietor, it not being in my power, under the tenure by which Dower Negroes are held, to manumit them. (*Last Will and Testament of George Washington of Mount Vernon*)

The only slave Washington freed at his death was his body servant William, "as a testimony of my sense of his attachment to me and for his faithful services during the Revolution" (Freeman, *George Washington*).

Washington's struggle with principle typified the internal conflict experienced by many of his contemporaries. Most of them, unlike Washington, abandoned the struggle without resolving it. Washington's bold step of acting on his principles, however, has long been revered by the black community. Although an heir to the institution of slavery, the father of our country set a proud example though posthumously ridding himself of it.

29-54

MOUNT ZION BAPTIST CHURCH

105 Ridge Street, Charlottesville

Virginia Landmarks Register, June 19, 1991
National Register of Historic Places, October 15, 1992

Charlottesville's Mount Zion Baptist Church evokes the struggle by the city's Afro-Americans to establish a viable community following emancipation. Determined to participate in mainstream society, black citizens felt it was important to do so in a manner compatible with their own needs, independent of white authority.

Fence detail, Mount Zion Baptist Church

Blacks required institutions that were truly their own, and the churches filled the need. The churches not only met the religious needs of their members but also served as social centers, theaters, and meeting places for dealing with the affairs of the black community.

The movement for independence from white authority in Charlottesville began before the close of the Civil War. In 1864 black Baptists, both free and slave, petitioned the white Baptist church for dismissal from the segregated galleries and moved toward establishing their own congregations. The congregation of the black First Baptist Church was organized in 1864. In 1867 the Mount Zion congregation was organized. Mount Zion's members first met in each other's homes until Samuel White, one of the flock, offered his Ridge Street house as a permanent meeting place. The group soon outgrew the house and in 1875 purchased a lot next door where it built a wooden church. The church was enlarged several times until 1883 when it was demolished to make way for the present church, completed in 1884, an imposing brick building which reflected the growing importance of Charlottesville's black community.

Charlottesville's black churches received the support of the local white establishment, who recognized that they were the vehicles by which blacks developed the leadership needed to encourage responsible citizenship. Churches were the primary means by which freedmen were prepared to participate in a new society. Indeed, the effectiveness of Charlottesville's black churches in this effort resulted in race relations far more congenial than in other parts of the South.

Mount Zion Baptist Church is typical of the church buildings erected by the more prosperous black congregations in Virginia towns. Local tradition has assigned its design to George Wallace Spooner, an architect who lived nearby and later participated in the rebuilding of the Rotunda at the University of Virginia following its fire. The contractor for the church was A. G. Wallace. Although the church has undergone various modifications over the years, its original architectural character is intact. Its dominant features are its solid brick walls and tall, pointed tower above the entrance. The church remains in regular use by the Mount Zion congregation.

104-181

J. THOMAS NEWSOME HOUSE

2803 Oak Avenue, Newport News

Virginia Landmarks Register, December 12, 1989
National Register of Historic Places, December 19, 1990

This rambling Queen Anne–style residence was the home of J. Thomas Newsome (1869–1942), one of Newport News's most respected black civic leaders. The house not only serves as a reminder of Newsome's celebrated career but stands as a symbol of the emergence of the black professional class in the Hampton Roads area during the early decades of the twentieth century. It was in this period of dramatic industrial growth that the Newport News Shipbuilding and Dry Dock Company rose to world eminence. The influx of black laborers to serve this enterprise spurred the development of a kindred professional community to meet their various needs.

Like many of the city's blacks, J. Thomas Newsome was raised in rural Virginia, in Sussex County. Unlike the majority of blacks, however, Newsome attended college, receiving an undergraduate degree from the Virginia Normal and Collegiate Institution (now Virginia State University). He then attended law school at Howard University where he graduated in 1899 as class valedictorian. Newsome's law practice, opened in Newport News, was distinguished and pathbreaking. He was an effective advocate of the rights of blacks, and in 1913 he became one of the first black lawyers to practice before the Virginia Supreme Court of Appeals.

Newsome is probably best remembered for his many and varied community efforts, a testament to his remarkable range of interests. He was instrumental in the founding of Trinity Baptist Church and served as the Sunday school superintendent for nineteen years. He was a leading advocate for the construction of Huntington High School and was also active in politics. It was during one of the low points of the black experience in America that Newsome busied himself unifying the black community of the area by organizing the Colored Voters League of Warwick County, an activity that gained him appointment as assistant sergeant-at-arms for the 1920 Republican National Convention. As editor of the city's

J. Thomas Newsome

Stair hall, J. Thomas Newsome house

black newspaper, the *Newport News Star,* he shaped public opinion and guided public action, particularly that of area blacks. At the time of his death just after the outbreak of World War II, Newsome was commissioner of chancery and a member of the Newport News Citizens Defense Policy Committee and the Hampton Roads Regional Defense Council.

Newsome purchased the large house on Oak Avenue in 1906. Begun in 1898, it originally was the home of Dr. William R. Granger who at the time was one of only two black physicians in the city. The house, with its gables, corner tower, and wraparound front porch, is typical of the larger residences that line the streets of southeastern Newport News, a by-product of the city's turn-of-the-century industrial prosperity. The property is now owned by the city of Newport News and is operated by the Newsome House Museum and Cultural Center, an organization formed to restore the house for use as a community center and museum, focusing on the black history of Newport News and the life of J. Thomas Newsome.

121-52

OLD CHRISTIANSBURG INDUSTRIAL INSTITUTE AND SCHAEFFER MEMORIAL BAPTIST CHURCH

570 High Street, Christiansburg

Virginia Landmarks Register, May 16, 1978
National Register of Historic Places, April 6, 1979

On a promontory overlooking the town of Christiansburg, the Old Christiansburg Industrial Institute and the Schaeffer Memorial Baptist Church, both built in 1885, are monuments of the social, educational, and religious history of the black community of Montgomery County. The institute traces its origins to 1866 when Captain Charles S. Schaeffer, an agent of the Freedmen's Bureau and later an ordained Baptist pastor, began formal instruction for the area's blacks. Schaeffer's work in this southwestern Virginia town marked an unusually early effort toward bringing former slaves in the region into the mainstream of American life. His school predated by several years the public school system established to serve the county's whites.

Captain Schaeffer emphasized technical, academic, and religious training at Christiansburg. Not long after starting the school, Schaeffer founded the Christiansburg African Baptist Church and used the church building both for religious worship and education. Schaeffer's institute prospered. By 1869 blacks were coming from long distances to attend classes. Quarters were provided in the rude cabins of local blacks or at the Schaeffer residence.

In 1873, with financial aid from the Quakers, a new school building was erected and used as a normal school. The institution soon outgrew these early structures. In 1885 an impressive brick church and an adjacent brick school building were constructed; Schaeffer himself assisted with the design. The school building, a two-story, solid brick structure known as the Hill School, was an unusually commodious facility for a southern black training school of the period. The church, dominated by its tall corner tower with steep pyramidal roof, instantly became one of the principal architectural landmarks of Christiansburg and could be seen from great distances. Later named the Schaeffer Memorial Baptist Church, it continues to function as a house of worship. Connected to the church is a small wood-frame annex, known as the Primary Annex, added in 1888, which contains a memorial window honoring Ada A. Schaeffer, wife of Captain Schaeffer.

In 1895 the school was reorganized under the direction of Booker T. Washington, who instituted a much-expanded curriculum. The newly shaped institute modeled its program on those pioneered at Hampton Institute and Tuskegee Institute. The expansion necessitated the acquisition of a new campus for the high school–level students in 1902. Industrial training continued at the Hill School until 1953. Since 1967 the school building, still the property of the Trustees of the Schaeffer Memorial Baptist Church, has been used as a community center.

60-85

OLD FIRST AFRICAN BAPTIST CHURCH

College Street at East Broad Street, Richmond

Virginia Landmarks Register, November 5, 1968
National Register of Historic Places, April 16, 1969

The former home of Richmond's oldest black Baptist congregation symbolizes the ascendancy of the city's blacks from the Civil War through the late nineteenth century. Between 1820 and 1860 Richmond was one of the most populous and successful industrial centers in the country. The main industry, tobacco, depended exclusively on black workers. Tobacco manufacturers generally owned many of their factory hands and hired free blacks to fill the rest of their labor needs. The slaves worked in the factories six days a week, and on the seventh they joined other slaves and free blacks for religious worship. The majority of the blacks, slave and free, in Richmond and elsewhere in the South were Baptists, and they vastly outnumbered the city's white Baptists. Baptist churches had racially mixed memberships, and black deacons, elected by the entire membership, assisted white pastors in ministering to the black members.

Antebellum Richmond's leading Baptist congregation, First Baptist, originally met in a church erected in 1802 at College and Broad streets. Although the church was integrated, the blacks of First Baptist, along with others of the city's black Baptists, continually petitioned for permission to establish churches of their own. In 1841 the white members of First Baptist built at Broad and Twelfth streets an

Old First African Baptist Church interior, circa 1928

First African Baptist Church Sunday school orchestra, 1928

imposing new church designed by the nationally prominent architect Thomas U. Walter. That same year the state legislature finally permitted the establishment of Richmond's first strictly black Baptist church. The congregation of First Baptist sold their old church to their black members, and the First African Baptist Church thus came into being. Although the new African church was independent, the law required that it have a white pastor, and Dr. Robert Ryland, first president of Richmond College, was nominated to be its spiritual leader. First African Baptist grew dramatically under Dr. Ryland's leadership, becoming the city's largest and most prestigious black Baptist church and serving as a model for three other pre–Civil War African Baptist churches.

With the fall of the Confederacy, blacks seized full control of their churches in

June 1865. They named their own pastors and used their buildings not only for worship but as places for offering education to their members. In 1876 the prospering First African Baptist congregation replaced the 1802 building with the present structure. In a gesture to its parent church, the new church was modeled after the 1841 First Baptist Church, employing a Greek Revival Doric portico *in muris*. A grand organ, purchased in 1886, enhanced the inspirational and extemporaneous singing for which the congregation was noted. First African Baptist remained at its historic location until 1955 when the property was sold to the Medical College of Virginia. The congregation purchased for its new home the former Barton Heights Baptist Church on the city's north side. The exterior of the Old First African Baptist building remains essentially unchanged while the sanctuary has been divided into two levels of offices.

127-167

The Crater, Petersburg National Military Park

PETERSBURG NATIONAL MILITARY PARK

Siege Road, Petersburg

Virginia Landmarks Register, October 18, 1983
National Register of Historic Places, October 15, 1966

The focal point of the Petersburg National Military Park is a large depression known as the Crater where, on July 30, 1864, black soldiers of the Union army exhibited exceptional heroism against an overwhelming Confederate defense. The Battle of the Crater marked one of the bloodiest encounters of the war in which blacks were engaged in combat.

The role of blacks in the Union fighting forces is an important but often over-looked aspect of Civil War history. At the onset of the war, the Union army reject-ed black citizens who attempted to enlist. Blacks served in both armies as laborers and servants, but not until 1862 did the U.S. Congress authorize President Lincoln to accept black soldiers. Following the issuance of the Emancipation Proclamation on January 1, 1863, large numbers of blacks enlisted in the Union army. During the war about two hundred thousand blacks served, mostly in the segregated units called U.S. Colored Troops (USCTs), which were commanded by white officers.

At first the USCTs were detailed as guards for wagon trains and other similar duties, but eventually they were allowed into combat. Before the war ended black troops had fought in all theaters in 449 engagements and had suffered more casu-alties than white troops, in part because some Confederates refused to take black prisoners.

The USCTs and other black units fought well once they were allowed in com-bat. During the Battle of New Market Heights on September 29, 1864, a part of the attack on Richmond's defenses known as the Battle of Chaffin's Farm or Fort Har-rison, black soldiers exhibited such valor that fourteen of them were later awarded the Medal of Honor. Only sixteen black soldiers were awarded the medal during the entire war.

In June and July 1864, during the siege of Petersburg, Union troops, in a dra-matic effort to break the Southern defense after a month of bombardment, tun-neled under the Confederate lines and planted four tons of gunpowder. At 4:45 A.M. on July 30 the powder was ignited. The spectacular explosion killed and maimed three hundred South Carolinians and created a crater 170 feet long, 60 to 80 feet wide, and 30 feet deep. Three divisions of white Union soldiers attacked, hoping to widen the breach, but Major General William Mahone rushed forward with a Confederate division and sealed the gap. At that juncture a division of black Union troops was ordered to charge into the crater. Floundering in the mangled earth, the division attempted unsuccessfully to scale the crater's sides and were slaughtered by the Confederates. Responsibility for the fiasco was assigned to the white generals in charge. The courage and tenacity of the black troops were ad-mired by soldiers on both sides.

The site of the Battle of the Crater is preserved in the Petersburg National Mili-tary Park. It is the only Civil War site in Virginia closely associated with black troops in combat that is presently listed in the state and national registers.

123-71

Phoenix Bank of Nansemond

PHOENIX BANK OF NANSEMOND

339 East Washington Street, Suffolk

Virginia Landmarks Register, August 21, 1990
National Register of Historic Places, January 24, 1991

The simple commercial building erected in 1921 to house the Phoenix Bank of Nansemond represents the effort of blacks in southeastern Virginia to establish, out of necessity, their own commercial enterprises. Because segregation laws prevented blacks from full participation in mercantile activities and because white-run banks resisted extending credit to them, black businessmen in the first decades of the century created lending institutions to serve their community. Between 1900 and 1920 twenty black banks opened in Virginia, half of them in the tidewater area. The Phoenix Bank of Nansemond was founded in 1919 primarily to serve the black laborers and farmers of Suffolk and the county of Nansemond (now part of the city of Suffolk).

During this period Suffolk was gaining recognition as the "Peanut Capital of the United States." This thriving industry brought economic gain to black workers both within Suffolk and on the surrounding farms. A full-service black business community including real estate offices, insurance agencies, shops, and undertakers developed on the east side of the railroad tracks in the racially divided city. The Phoenix Bank of Nansemond came into being inauspiciously around 1917 as a group of local men lending money to fellow blacks on an informal basis. The group attracted the attention of black physician, Dr. W. T. Fuller, who suggested that they were doing so well, they should form a proper bank. The bank was duly founded with Fuller being elected its first president.

The Phoenix Bank prospered from the beginning and was described by local blacks as "one of the most progressive banks of which the race can boast" (*Norfolk Journal and Guide,* February 12, 1921). At Dr. Fuller's death in 1921, John W. Richardson, the bank's vice-president, took over. Richardson was greatly admired in Suffolk. He gained local fame by simultaneously serving as president of the Phoenix Bank and janitor of the white-run American Bank and Trust Company, a feat which earned him a mention in a 1940 "Ripley's Believe It or Not" column. Richardson was also listed in *Who's Who in Colored America.* It was under Richardson's guidance that the bank's new building was erected on East Washington Street. Though compact, the building, with its terrazzo-floored lobby, seven offices, and second-floor apartments, was a point of pride. The vault was described as "second to none in the city as to security" (*Norfolk Journal and Guide,* May 28, 1921).

The Phoenix Bank of Nansemond operated until 1931 when it closed from lack of depositors, a victim of the Great Depression. The building, now vacant, most recently was used as a Chinese restaurant, and nearly all the original interior fittings, including the vault, have been removed. The parapet, however, still boasts a stone plaque reading "Phoenix Bank of Nansemond 1921," a reminder of the days when blacks had to support fellow blacks as well as the business fabric of their community by creating their own financial institutions.

133-86

Virginia Afro-American farm worker of the 1930s

PITTSYLVANIA COUNTY COURTHOUSE

Chatham, Pittsylvania County

Virginia Landmarks Register, June 16, 1981
National Register of Historic Places, October 29, 1981
National Historic Landmark, May 4, 1987

This antebellum Virginia courthouse represents a milestone in the blacks' struggle for civil rights in the post-Civil War era. It was at the Pittsylvania County court-house, in 1878, that Judge J. D. Coles attempted to use his authority to exclude blacks from serving as grand and petit jurors. As a result of his action, Judge Coles was arrested and charged with a violation of the Civil Rights Act of 1875. The judge filed a petition with the U.S. Supreme Court asking that charges be dropped on the grounds that his arrest and imprisonment were not warranted by the Constitution and the laws of the United States. The Supreme Court, in the case of *Ex parte Virginia*, held that Judge Coles's action did violate both the Civil Rights Act of 1875 and the equal protection clause of the Fourteenth Amendment to the U.S. Constitution.

Ex parte Virginia marks one of the few victories for blacks in federal court in the generation after 1865. It demonstrated that the Fourteenth and Fifteenth amendments indeed had resulted in the extension of national power for the protection of personal liberty and civil rights. While states retained the primary responsibility and power to regulate civil rights, they were no longer autonomous. *Ex parte Virginia* thus showed that the federal government had the qualified but potentially effective power to protect the rights of all citizens. Only a few years after the ruling, the U.S. Supreme Court in 1883 struck down the Civil Rights Act of 1875. Thus blacks, little aided by the courts and abandoned by the legislative and executive branches of the federal government, found the issue of civil rights largely absent from the national agenda until the 1950s. Though *Ex parte Virginia* represented the promise of the future, the struggle for full civil rights for blacks and other minorities, through both court and legislative action, had scarcely begun.

The courthouse in which Judge Coles attempted to restrict the rights of the county's black citizens is the principal landmark of the historic town of Chatham. Completed in 1853, the courthouse was designed and built by Sidney Shumaker, a local master builder. Typical of Virginia's mid-nineteenth-century court structures, the Greek Revival building has a quiet, understated dignity. The diminutive red-brick structure is fronted by a Doric portico, above which is an ornamental clock tower. Of particular interest is the well-preserved courtroom and its unusually elaborate plasterwork, little changed from the time of Judge Coles. The monument to the Confederate dead on the narrow lawn in front stands as an ironic counterpoint for this landmark in the history of black civil rights.

187-7

PRESTWOULD

Clarkesville Vicinity, Mecklenburg County

Virginia Landmarks Register, November 5, 1968
National Register of Historic places, October 1, 1969

The Mecklenburg County plantation developed for Sir Peyton Skipwith and Jean Miller Skipwith after their marriage in 1788 was among the largest in the state and boasted on the most elaborate building complexes of early republican Virginia. Records kept by Lady Skipwith offer important glimpses of Afro-American Slave life at Prestwould, and subsequent Skipwith papers provide unusually rich documentation about late antebellum slave families. The records offer the opportunity to study Afro-American individuals and families whose lives were intertwined with the Skipwiths'. A diverse group of buildings in which black people lived and worked survived at Prestwould into this century, and three of the buildings still stand. Among them is a 1790s slave house, an early plantation store converted to workers' housing after the Civil War, and a circa 1825 loom house with slaves' rooms upstairs.

The wood-frame slave house is the last standing building at the home quarter, and area shown as occupied by roughly nine houses on a 1796 plat of Prestwould. This quarter continued as the site of agricultural workers' houses into the present century. The surviving house is considered by architectural scholars to be the earliest known slave house in Virginia and perhaps the South. It is important not just as an oddity but as a rare and informative survival from a century in which slave housing was universally inferior even to the relatively low expectations of the late eighteenth century. The importance of the building was demonstrated by its use as

Prestwould slave house undergoing restoration, 1992

a design source for the recently re-created slave quarter at Carter's Grove, a project of the Colonial Williamsburg Foundation. The Prestwould slave house has also been included in a British Broadcasting Company film on the archaeology and public presentation of slavery.

The slave house began as a modest single-room structure measuring 12 feet by 16 feet covered with split clapboards rather the more regular sawn siding. About 1820, with a new generation of Skipwiths living at Prestwould, the house was substantially remodeled as a duplex quarter of the variety that became conventional throughout the South by the middle of the nineteenth century. The old room was expanded, another room for a second family was added, and a new central chimney was constructed. Glass windows were installed and sawn weatherboards added to the frame.

Little further change occurred to the building until after the Civil War when it and at least one other duplex quarter at Prestwould were converted to single-family houses. By 1991 the quarter was in a state of advanced decay. That same year it was stabilized and carefully restored with the assistance of experts from the Colonial Williamsburg Foundation. Now complete and exhibited to the public, this rare historic relic, a building evocative of the ignoble side of Virginia plantation life, stands in striking contrast to the elegance and refinement of the recently restored mansion interior. Prestwould in maintained as a privately administered museum complex owned by the Prestwould Foundation.

58-45, 46, 47

VIRGINIA RANDOLPH COTTAGE

2200 Mountain Road, Henrico County

Virginia Landmarks Register, March 18, 1975
National Historic Landmark, December 2, 1974

The plain brick cottage at the Virginia Randolph Educational Center is maintained as a memorial to a black woman who gained national repute for promoting innovative teaching methods among her people. In 1908 the Henrico County training school instructor Virginia Estelle Randolph (1874–1958), daughter of parents born slaves, was appointed the nation's first Jeanes supervising industrial

Virginia Estelle Randolph

teacher. The Jeanes supervisor was the outgrowth of an idea of a wealthy Philadelphia Quaker, Anna T. Jeanes, to establish a fund to employ black supervisors to
upgrade vocational training in black public schools in the South.

Virginia Randolph graduated from Richmond Normal School in 1890 at age
sixteen and immediately embarked on a teaching career which would last the rest
of her life. After teaching in Goochland County for two years, she took a position
at the Mountain Road School in Henrico County. Her effectiveness soon caught
the attention of Jackson T. Davis, the first superintendent of instruction for blacks
in the county. Davis was so impressed with Miss Randolph's teaching that he
sought funds to send her to schools throughout the county where she could train
other teachers in her methods. Davis's quest for funds eventually brought him into
contact with Dr. James H. Dillard, director of the fund established by the will of

Anna T. Jeanes. The resources of this relatively new fund had not been tapped, and Dr. Dillard determined that sponsoring Virginia Randolph to upgrade to training of teachers in the county's black elementary and secondary schools would be an appropriate first use of the fund.

The approach used by Miss Randolph generally followed the educational concepts employed by General Samuel C. Armstrong and Booker T. Washington at Hampton Institute and Tuskegee, where emphasis was placed on vocationalism. In addition to the three Rs, black students would learn domestic functions such as gardening, cooking, and sewing, as well as various trades such as woodworking and masonry. Miss Randolph recognized that if black youth were to achieve self-

1937 home economics class, Mountain Road School

sufficiency in a society from which they previously had been excluded, they had to be equipped with a variety of fundamental skills. To achieve this goal, however, it was necessary first to create a force of appropriately trained instructors.

The program became institutionalized under the sponsorship of the Negro Rural School Fund, the formal title of the Jeanes fund, and the idea spread throughout the South and eventually to countries in Africa, Asia, and Latin America. Virginia Randolph and her Henrico Plan thus became a model for thousands of teacher supervisors who followed.

Throughout her career Miss Randolph maintained an interest in Mountain Road School where she first worked in the 1890s. While serving as a Jeanes supervisor, she continued to teach at Mountain Road School until her retirement in 1949. The school eventually closed and was reestablished in 1969 as the Virginia Randolph Education Center. The 1939 cottage where Miss Randolph taught home economics and had her office converted into a museum honoring the distinguished educator, who is buried on the grounds in front.

43–43

RICHMOND ALMSHOUSE, WEST BUILDING

206 Hospital Street, Richmond

Virginia Landmarks Register, August 15, 1989
(included by amendment of the Richmond Almshouse nomination of July 21, 1981)
National Register of Historic Places, June 13, 1990
(included by amendment of the Richmond Almshouse nomination of October 29, 1981)

The original building of the Richmond Almshouse was erected in 1860–61 as a place of refuge for indigent whites. The impressive Italianate structure designed by city engineer Washington Gill was an outgrowth of the reform movement of the antebellum period. Such institutions were rare in the South since the spirit of reform was frequently associated with abolitionism, and southerners tended to keep themselves aloof from the zealous efforts of their northern contemporaries. Richmonders shared in this lack of enthusiasm for reform issues, but by the late 1850s the need to accommodate its growing poor white population could no longer be ignored. With the outbreak of the Civil War, the barely completed structure was converted to a military hospital and later served as temporary quarters for the Virginia Military Institute. After the war the almshouse finally was used to house poor people; by then laws enacted to maintain racial segregation in public institutions meant that the almshouse remained for whites only.

In contrast to the antebellum period, Virginia, along with most of the rest of the country, was profoundly influenced by the Progressive movement that developed at the turn of the twentieth century. In 1900 the Virginia Conference of Charities and Corrections was formed. The social awakening emerging from this Progressive-era activity made clear the necessity of meeting the needs of Richmond's penurious blacks. Thus in 1908 the City Council authorized the construction of a home for the city's "poor Negroes." This new building, a long, fully modern, two-story brick structure, was built immediately to the west of the 1861 almshouse. A description of the expanded complex appearing in the first annual report (1909) of the State Board of Charities and Corrections showed that Richmond had the largest and most impressive almshouse for blacks in the state.

Although segregation of the races was upheld without question at the Richmond Almshouse through separate living quarters, the blacks' accommodations were kept to high standards. The new building was equipped with modern conveniences such as steam heat, gas or electric lights, running water and indoor plumbing. Religious services were held several times a week, and some entertainment was provide, including visits to downtown.

By the late 1970s the Hospital Street complex, including the west building, by then known as the Richmond Nursing Home, an integrated facility, had become outdated. The occupants were moved to a more modern city-run nursing home, and the buildings were sold to developers for conversion to apartments for low-income elderly residents. The 1861 building was made available to tenants by 1985. The west building was rehabilitated and occupied five years later. Despite the stigma of segregation, the west building of the former Richmond Almshouse represents a conspicuous early effort on behalf of the former capital of the Confederacy to deal with the welfare of its dependent black citizens.

127-353

ST. JOHN'S AFRICAN METHODIST EPISCOPAL CHURCH

539-545 East Bute Street, Norfolk

Virginia Landmarks Register, October 14, 1986
National Register of Historic Places, December 4, 1986

The completion of St. John's A.M.E. Church in 1888 symbolized the beginning of a period of ascendancy for Norfolk's black congregations. The church was the first of a series of architecturally sophisticated, if not assertive, black religious edifices to adorn the city. These buildings in no way were inferior in size or quality of design to any of the city's white churches. St. John's and the subsequent black

Ceiling trusses, St. John's A.M.E. Church

churches thus were remarkable achievements considering the fact that many of the churches' members had been born slaves and were mostly of modest means.

Because there were few, if any, trained black architects in Virginia in the late nineteenth century, the black congregations had to rely on white firms. The congregation of St. John's started the trend of Norfolk blacks selecting not second-rate but leading firms to design their houses of worship. The architect chosen for St. John's was Charles M. Cassell, one of the most respected Norfolk architects of the period. Writing in 1888 Robert W. Lamb stated in *Our Twin Cities of the Nineteenth Century, Norfolk and Portsmouth:* "the largest church edifice erected by our colored people will be, however, the St. John's A.M.E. Church, situated on Bute Street, near Church Street. The cornerstone of the new church, now being built on the site of the old one by Mssrs. Tee and Brittingham, was laid April 16, 1888. Under the supervision of Mr. Cassell, one of our city's excellent architects, the work is being rapidly pushed and will be completed this year making a very handsome addition to the architecture of this part of the city."

Stylistically, St. John's is a bold representative in red brick of the Romanesque Revival idiom, popularized in America by the architect II. II. Richardson. Typical of the style, the facade employs asymmetrical towers and a multiplicity of round-arch openings. One of the highlights of the exterior is the large central stained-glass memorial incorporating an elaborate rose window in the upper portion. Perhaps the most striking feature of the church is the sanctuary's hammer-beam ceiling, a remarkable demonstration of medieval-style timber framing.

The history of St. John's congregation closely parallels the social evolution of Norfolk's blacks from slavery to freedom. The congregation began as a mission for slaves organized around 1800 by the Cumberland Street Methodist Episcopal Church. It obtained its independence in 1863 under the authority of the Union forces' martial law then governing the city. It joined the A.M.E. connection in 1864 and prospered thereafter to the point that it was able to erect the largest nineteenth-century black church in Norfolk. The Twenty-third Quadrennial Session of the A.M.E. Church was held at St. John's in May 1908 during which event five bishops were consecrated. In 1989 St. John's became the first church in the Commonwealth to be protected through a Virginia Board of Historic Resources preservation easement.

122-211

ST. LUKE BUILDING

900 St. James Street, Richmond

Virginia Landmarks Register, April 21, 1981
National Register of Historic Places, September 16, 1982

The St. Luke Building was erected to house the national headquarters of the Independent Order of St. Luke, a black benevolent society founded in Baltimore in 1867 by Mary Prout, a former slave. Like similar benevolent societies, the St. Luke grew from the buying societies of the antebellum period to an organization offering guidance and financial aid to struggling freedmen. The society served to bridge the gap between bondage and freedom: easing the burdens of illness and death, encouraging savings and thrift, providing an outlet for inexpensive but well-made retail goods, and promoting black self-sufficiency.

The society struggled with minimal assets until 1899 when the pioneering black businesswoman, philanthropist, and educator, Mrs. Maggie L. Walker, became the organization's Right Worthy Grand Secretary. Born in 1867 to an ex-slave, Mrs. Walker taught school before becoming involved with the society. She was instrumental in having its headquarters established in Richmond. Her able administration and reorganization of the society's affairs increased its membership from less than a thousand to twenty thousand within seven years. Under her auspices the society established the St. Luke Penny Savings Bank, of which she was president. This bank, after several mergers, became the Consolidated Bank and Trust Company, one of the few black banks to survive the Great Depression. Other activities

Maggie L. Walker (at back) and coworkers at the St. Luke Building

of the order included the operation of a department store known as the St. Luke Emporium and the publication of the *St. Luke Herald,* a weekly magazine which encouraged thrift and regular savings.

In 1903 the order's headquarters was moved from Church Hill to the present building at 900 St. James Street in Jackson Ward. The new headquarters, another of Mrs. Walker's projects, was a bold architectural statement for a black organization. They chose a white Richmond architect, Peter J. White, who styled it to inspire confidence and stability. By 1915 the flourishing society needed more space, and the St. Luke Building received two additional floors, the project being directed by Professor Charles T. Russell of Virginia Union University. In the society's heyday the first floor housed shops, the second and third floors were large, flexible spaces used for meetings, and the top floor contained the order's offices. In the basement was the printing room for the *St. Luke Herald.*

The Independent Order of St. Luke served the black community for more than a century. By the 1980s many of its services were no longer needed or were being offered by other institutions, and the order was finally disbanded. The building still provides benefit to Richmond's blacks through its current use as the headquarters of the Richmond Community Action Program.

127-352

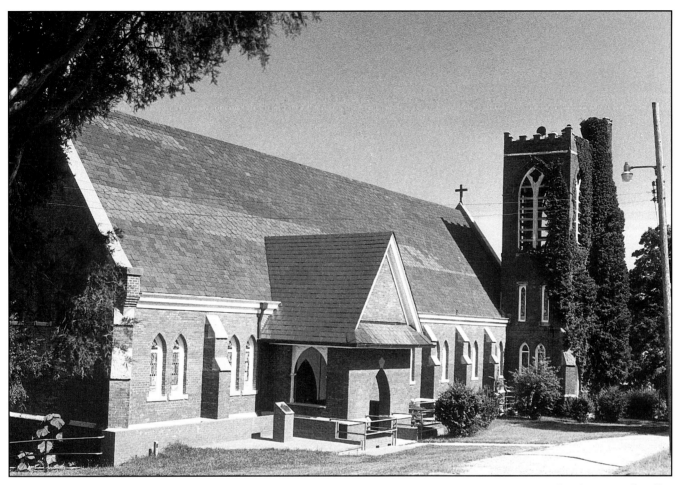

Chapel, Saint Paul's College

SAINT PAUL'S COLLEGE

Lawrenceville, Brunswick County

Virginia Landmarks Register, March 20, 1979
National Register of Historic Places, June 27, 1979

Saint Paul's College grew out of the faith and labor of the Reverend James Solomon Russell (1857–1935), a black Episcopal priest who recognized the importance of providing higher education with a spiritual basis to the rural blacks of post–Civil War Virginia. Russell was born into slavery in Mecklenburg County in 1857 and was educated at Hampton Institute. He became interested in the Episcopal church and decided to enter the ministry. He studied for the priesthood at a branch of the Virginia Theological Seminary in Petersburg set up specifically for his training. This branch later was formally established as the Bishop Payne Divinity School for the purpose of training black Episcopal priests. Assigned to

The Reverend James Solomon Russell

Lawrenceville as a deacon, Russell, as he stated in his autobiography, *Adventure in Faith* (1936), found black communicants without a church in a community where "race prejudice seemed rampant and public opinion indifferent if not actually hostile." By February 1883 he had succeeded in constructing a chapel for black worshipers. He soon organized a parochial school, and classes were held in the chapel vestry room.

The need to expand educational opportunities for the area's blacks soon became evident. With funds contributed by the Reverend James Saul of Philadelphia, Russell and his parishioners built a three-room frame school building. Named the Saul Building in honor of its benefactor, this simple structure became the genesis of Saint Paul's Normal and Industrial School, founded by Russell in 1888. The school was later formally incorporated by act of the General Assembly, and the first meeting of Saint Paul's board of trustees was held in 1893.

Saint Paul's rapid growth was evidenced in the construction of classroom and dormitory buildings. In 1900 a commodious Queen Anne–style residence for the school principal was added to the complex. The first brick building on the campus was the school chapel, a handsome Gothic-style structure built in 1904, largely with student labor. The chapel's construction was made possible by a donation from the Diocese of Long Island given in memory of Katherine Van Rensselaer Delafield.

The school's increased enrollment of pupils from outside the Brunswick County vicinity resulted in an expanded curriculum for the school. Liberal arts courses were developed, and a department of teacher training was added in 1922. Degree programs leading the Bachelor of Science and the Bachelor of Science in Education were started in 1942. In 1957 the school's name was changed to Saint Paul's College. Today the college, with an enrollment of more than six hundred, is nonsectarian and open to all races. While not church-controlled, it remains affiliated with the Episcopal church and one of only three historically black Episcopal colleges in the country. The Saul Building, the principal's house (now the Fine Arts Building), and the chapel constitute the historic core of the institution.

251-3

Auto mechanics class, 1939, Saint Paul's College

ANNE SPENCER HOUSE

1313 Pierce Street, Lynchburg

Virginia Landmarks Register, September 21, 1976
National Register of Historic Places, December 6, 1976

During her long and active life, Anne Spencer (1882–1975) was recognized by her friends and associates as a lyric poet of considerable talent. For a black woman to win recognition from her intellectual peers was a remarkable feat given the climate of the times. Through quiet determination and dedication to her craft and causes, she gained respect not only as a gifted writer but as an educator and humanitarian. Her devotion to cultural enlightenment for blacks was expressed in her position as a librarian and teacher, as well as in the lively rapport she maintained with

Anne Spencer

Edankraal interior, Anne Spencer house

many of the nation's most noted black leaders. Through correspondence and conversation the vigorous minds of these individuals were tempered by Anne Spencer's gentle but firm notions on the advancement of her race.

Anne Spencer openly expressed her intolerance of bigotry and oppression of blacks and women, but she rarely used her poetical works as a vehicle for social protest. Rather, her poems dwell mainly on the more universal themes of love and respect for beauty, truth, nature, and the human spirit. Because she wrote for personal insight rather than monetary gain, only a few of her poems have been published. It was at the insistence of her friend and fellow poet James Weldon Johnson that several of her poems, including "At the Carnival," "Questing," and "Lines to a Nasturtium," were submitted and subsequently appeared in major poetry anthologies. Her personal philosophy and attitude toward her station in life were summed up when she wrote: "I write about the things I love. I have no civilized articulation for the things I hate. I proudly love being a Negro Woman—it's so involved and interesting. We are the PROBLEM—the great national game TABOO" (J. Lee Greene, *Time's Unfading Garden*).

Anne Bannister Spencer was born on a plantation in Henry County. Although she was eleven before she could read and write, she was valedictorian of her class at the Virginia Seminary and Normal School in Lynchburg in 1899. In 1901 she married classmate Edward Alexander Spencer, and in 1903 they moved into their new home at 1313 Pierce Street. This commodious house, largely built by her husband, remained Anne Spencer's residence until her death. He also built the garden cottage as a place where Ann could write and think in privacy. The name of the cottage, Edankraal, was the combination of an anagram of the Spencer's first names and an African word for enclosure or refuge.

For many years 1313 Pierce Street was a place of hospitality and pilgrimage for prominent Afro-Americans. In the days when there were few public accommodations for blacks in the South, homes such as the Spencers' were welcome stopping places. Among Anne Spencer's visitors were such luminaries as George Washington Carver, W. E. B. Du Bois, Langston Hughes, Martin Luther King, Jr., Thurgood Marshall, Adam Clayton Powell, Jr., and Paul Robeson. The property is now owned and exhibited by the Friends of Anne Spencer Memorial Foundation, Inc.

118-61

STANTON FAMILY CEMETERY

Diana Mills Vicinity, Buckingham County

Virginia Landmarks Register, February 17, 1993
National Register of Historic Places, April 29, 1993

Started in 1853, the Stanton family cemetery in rural Buckingham County is one of the state's few surviving burying grounds established by free blacks before the Civil War and held by the same family to the present. The Stanton family, whose members are recorded as free blacks as early as 1820, was one of the few extended free black families living in rural Virginia at the height of the slavery period. The 1840 census of Buckingham County recorded only 139 free blacks compared with 11,441 slaves, a proportional imbalance typical throughout the state. The family's progenitors, Nancy Stanton and her husband Daniel, formalized their social and economic status in 1853 when they purchased a forty-six acre tract to farm. Farming one's own property was especially esteemed among blacks; only 35 percent of free blacks rented or owned land. Nancy Stanton died of bilious colic the same year she and Daniel acquired their land and became the first of the Stantons to be interred in the cemetery.

The acreage of the Stanton farm was increased to its present size of ninety acres in the latter part of the nineteenth century by Sidney Trent Stanton, Sr., younger son of Nancy and Daniel Stanton. Although the family had moved from the homestead by 1930, it retained ownership of the land and the cemetery and continued family burials there. The last burial occurred in 1941 when Harriet Stanton Scott, granddaughter of Nancy and Daniel Stanton, was interred.

Today the 68-foot by 65-foot unfenced plot contains at least thirty-six marked burials, a large number for Afro-American family cemeteries. It likely holds additional unmarked burials. The cemetery layout features six rows spaced from one to five feet apart, varying in size from two to nine irregularly spaced graves. Many of the marked graves have simple uninscribed slate headstones and footstones. Three marble headstones mark the graves of World War I veterans. All of the graves are oriented on an east-west axis, an old tradition particularly associated with Afro-American cemeteries.

The slate for the markers came from the nearby Buckingham slate quarries where early in the present century Sidney Trent Stanton, Jr., worked as a quarryman. Stanton was also a skilled carpenter and may have made some of the coffins in which family members were buried. The fourteen children reared by Stanton and his wife Znada at the Buckingham farm were probably the first formally educated generation of Stantons. After Stanton's death in a quarry explosion in 1929, most of the children eventually left the homestead for greater opportunities in the North. The house disappeared save for its foundation, and the cemetery was left untended. Maintenance has been resumed in recent years. In 1990 the Stanton family placed near the cemetery entrance a slate monument honoring Daniel and Nancy Stanton.

14-52

THIRD STREET BETHEL AFRICAN METHODIST EPISCOPAL CHURCH

614 North Third Street, Richmond

Virginia Landmarks Register, February 18, 1975
National Register of Historic Places, June 5, 1975

This downtown Richmond landmark is one of the state's very few surviving black churches erected before the Civil War. It was at this church, in 1867, that the Virginia Conference of the African Methodist Episcopal church was formed. The congregation was organized in 1850 by the black members of the Trinity Methodist

Church, then located on Franklin Street and Locust Alley. In 1856 the flourishing body erected a simple brick sanctuary, the main portion of the present building, in the heart of Jackson Ward, a neighborhood then populated largely by Germans. Much of the labor for the construction was supplied by slaves.

The African Methodist Episcopal denomination originated in Philadelphia in 1784, when Richard Allen, a black Methodist, became dissatisfied with the mainstream church and left to form his own church. In 1816 he organized the first conference of African Methodist Episcopal churches, again in Philadelphia. In the slave states, however, black Methodists could not as easily forsake white supervision. All-black congregations remained under the control of the white Methodist Episcopal church until after the outbreak of the Civil War. In conformance with

Third Street Bethel A.M.E. Church, circa 1890

Virginia law, the Third Street Methodist Church's first pastor, G. W. Nolley, was white.

The first congregation to enter the African Methodist Episcopal fold in Virginia was that of the Bute Street Methodist Church of Norfolk, now St. John's A.M.E. Church, which in 1863 joined the Baltimore Conference. At the urging of the Norfolk church, a conference was convened at the Third Street Church in Richmond on May 10, 1867, and there the Virginia Conference of the A.M.E. church was organized, with Bishop Alexander Washington Wayman presiding. Third Street Church formally entered the A.M.E. connection at that time and added "Bethel" to its name, in honor of the mother church in Philadelphia. The Reverend J. S. D. Hall was the church's first conference-appointed pastor.

The congregation prospered, and in 1875 the exterior of the plain brick church was embellished with the addition of a pressed-brick facade incorporating two Gothic towers. Further remodeling took place under the supervision of architect Carl Ruehrmund in 1914 when the sanctuary was altered, the front stairs to the sanctuary entrance were added, and pediments were added to the towers. The work was completed in time for the church to serve as the site of the semicentennial of the Virginia Annual A.M.E. Conference, held on May 10, 1916. Third Street Bethel has continued to the present as a leading religious institution in Jackson Ward. In recent years it has joined the Downtown Community Ministry, an association made up of the leading downtown churches, formed to address the needs of the city's poor and homeless.

127-274

WILLIAM H. TRUSTY HOUSE

76 West County Street, Hampton

Virginia Landmarks Register, February 26, 1979
National Register of Historic Places, June 22, 1979

The stylish late Victorian house built in 1897 for William H. Trusty stands as a reminder of the new sense of political, social, and economic freedom enjoyed by Virginia's blacks in the decades following emancipation. Born in 1862 of freed parents in Prince George County, William H. Trusty rose from his humble origins to become a successful businessman and civic leader. His effectiveness in community

William H. Trusty

affairs was demonstrated in 1901 when he was elected to the council for the newly formed town of Phoebus, now part of the city of Hampton.

The Trusty family moved to the Hampton vicinity around 1871. Like many of Virginia's rural blacks, they were attracted to the area because of the proximity of Fort Monroe. The Freedmens' Bureau and Hampton Institute had made it a haven and place of opportunity for former slaves. With the influx of black immigrants, the black population of the region soon outnumbered the whites, especially in the former Elizabeth City County's Phoebus neighborhood, which was immediately adjacent to Fort Monroe.

Trusty, adhering to the philosophy of self-help espoused by such black leaders as Booker T. Washington, through thrift and diligence accumulated capital and purchased property in Phoebus. By age sixteen he was working for one of the merchants who kept a store at Fort Monroe. He gained social prominence by joining and participating in various black social and religious organizations. At age thirty-two he married Bera Franklin.

Phoebus was incorporated as a town in 1900. Trusty's election to town's first council made him one of the first blacks to be so elected in a Virginia municipality. At the time of his election, Trusty was self-employed. He operated his own bar on Mallory Street, owned five houses and two Main Street business properties, and lived in a fine new Victorian residence erected in 1897 for himself and his wife on West County Street, then called Shell Road. His house, constructed by P. A. Fuller of Fuller & Morgan, was the most expensive in the neighborhood. Its jauntily projecting two-level porch with spindle friezes and shingled railing made it especially conspicuous.

Trusty was unable to enjoy the fruits of his success for he died suddenly in 1902 at the age of forty. The house passed to Trusty's widow and eventually was occupied by her sister-in-law. It fell into serious disrepair but became the focus of preservation interests in 1976 when the neighborhood was targeted for urban renewal. Through the diligent efforts of the late Mrs. Sandidge Evans, noted Hampton preservationist, the house was expertly restored and is now used as rental property.

114-108

TRUXTUN HISTORIC DISTRICT
Portsmouth

Virginia Landmarks Register, April 15, 1980
National Register of Historic Places, September 16, 1982

Truxtun was the nation's first wartime government housing project constructed
exclusively for blacks. Named for Thomas Truxtun, an early naval hero, the forty-
two-acre neighborhood of 250 houses was developed in 1918 to accommodate the
growing workforce of blacks at the Norfolk Naval Shipyard. Truxtun exhibits the
high planning standards of the U.S. Housing Corporation, the federal agency that
financed and built the community as a model village for the workers and their
families. The principal architect of the project was Rossel Edward Mitchell of Norfolk. H. P. Kelsey served as the chief planner.

The expansion of activity at the Norfolk Naval Shipyard following America's
entry into World War I all but depleted the supply of available housing in

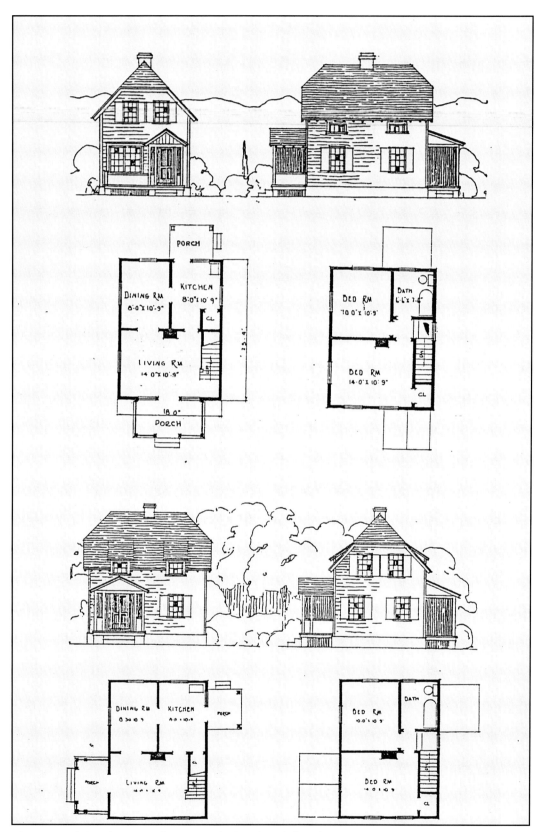

Elevations and plans for Truxtun houses, Rossel Edward Mitchell, architect

Portsmouth. To provide for the white workers, the U.S. Housing Corporation planned and built Cradock, an essentially self-contained neighborhood of more than seven hundred dwellings. Truxtun, called by L. K. Sherman, president of the housing corporation, "an experiment that will be watched" (*Portsmouth Star,* May 28, 1919), represented a pioneering effort on behalf of blacks. The decision to segregate the two projects accorded with federal policy established in the Wilson administration.

Truxtun's residences consisted of fifty duplexes and two hundred detached houses of five rooms each. The close-knit structures came in four basic styles. Their roof shapes and porches were arranged on the street fronts so that the eye met changing forms rather than a tiresome repetition. At a time when many urban blacks were living in primitive conditions, the project's houses boasted indoor plumbing and electric lights. Other planning innovations included spacing the houses eleven feet apart to allow for air flow and ventilation. The secondary roads were laid out east-west to give access to the prevailing winds. Utility poles were placed behind the houses rather than in front. Varying setbacks and a planting strip between the sidewalks and roadbed assured greenspace. Additional greenspace was provided by a large triangle between two major street that was designated as public open space. The original plan called for a church, a community house, and a school at the principal intersection. Of these, only the school was realized.

Although most of the houses have undergone minor alterations since the 1920s, only two of the original dwellings have been lost. Truxtun maintains a high degree of neighborhood pride. Confirmation of that pride came in 1979 when the residents supported the designation of the neighborhood as a local historic district by the city of Portsmouth, bringing with it special zoning to protect the area from inappropriate changes.

124-47

Vawter Hall

VAWTER HALL AND OLD PRESIDENT'S HOUSE

College Avenue, Virginia State University, Ettrick, Chesterfield County

---

Virginia Landmarks Register, February 19, 1980
National Register of Historic Places, May 7, 1980

Vawter Hall and the old President's House, the two oldest buildings at Virginia State University, make up the historic core of the oldest state-supported college for blacks in the United States. The school was chartered in 1882 as the Virginia Normal and Collegiate Institute to fulfill a pledge of the Readjuster party, led by former Confederate general William Mahone, to establish a state institute for higher learning for blacks. It was due in part to the black vote that the Readjusters had been successful in overthrowing Virginia's entrenched Democratic party. The bill to establish the school was introduced and pushed to passage by Mahone's lieutenant, Alfred W. Harris, of Petersburg, one of the thirteen blacks serving in the Virginia House of Delegates in 1882. The school's charter called for an all-black board and an all-black faculty.

Upon opening, the school divided its offerings between teacher training and a general liberal arts program which included classics, higher mathematics, and other humanities. With the fall from power of the Readjuster party a few years later, the school was caught in the cross fire of politics. Whites replaced blacks on the board, appropriations were cut, and faculty reduced. Appointed president in 1888, James H. Johnston, Sr., sought to isolate the college from the political climate. Subscribing to the accommodationist policies of Booker T. Washington, Johnston introduced vocational training to the curriculum, using this shift in emphasis as a means of demonstrating to politicians that the school was rendering valuable service to the total community.

Virginia State University 1939 home economics class

In 1908 Johnston was successful in getting the school's annual state appropriation of $20,000 restored. That same year construction was completed on Vawter Hall, a large brick building to house the school's vocational education classrooms. The building was named for Charles E. Vawter, the school's late rector and an authority on industrial training. Petersburg architect Harrison Waite designed the H-shaped structure. Vawter Hall was built in conjunction with the adjacent president's house, authorized by the board of trustees in 1906. Waite probably designed this modified Queen Anne–style dwelling as well. The two buildings supplemented the later-demolished Virginia Hall of 1888, the first building erected for the school.

In 1920 the school became the state's land grant college for blacks. In 1946 its name was changed to Virginia State College, and in 1979 it was renamed Virginia State University. Among its distinguished alumni was William H. Lewis, the first black to be named to an All-American football team and to hold a subcabinet post, serving as assistant attorney general to President Taft; Camilla Williams, the first black to star in a major opera company; Hugh Smyth, one of the nation's first black ambassadors; and Alfred Cade, one of our first black generals. Although historically a black institution, Virginia State University is today open to all races.

333-64

Hayes Hall (demolished)

VIRGINIA COLLEGE AND VIRGINIA SEMINARY
DeWitt Street, Lynchburg

Virginia Landmarks Register, February 26, 1979
National Register of Historic Places, June 19, 1979

The educational institution now known as Virginia College and Virginia Seminary is one of several Virginia schools of higher education founded in the late nineteenth century to help bring the state's blacks into the mainstream of society. The school traces its origins to the nineteenth session of the Virginia Baptist Convention, held in May 1886 at the First Baptist Church in Lexington. The Reverend P. F. Morris, pastor of Lynchburg's Court Street Baptist Church, offered the resolution that authorized the establishment of what was first known as the Lynchburg Baptist Seminary.

The school opened in January 1980 with thirty-three students. Its first brick building, begun in 1888, was a large and imposing structure in the Second Empire style, containing classrooms, a recitation hall, and dormitories. The three-and-a-half-story structure was reminiscent of Virginia Hall (1874) at Hampton Institute and was likely inspired by it. The building was later named Hayes Hall in honor of Professor Gregory Willis Hayes, who became the second president of the institution. Hayes espoused the self-help principles for blacks advocated by Booker T. Washington. Under his direction the school became a pioneer in the field of black education, placing its primary emphasis on the training of teachers and ministers for work within the black community. A bust of Gregory Willis Hayes is located in a small landscaped garden on the school grounds.

The school has undergone several name changes and organizations in its century of existence. In 1900 it was renamed Virginia Theological Seminary and College. The college and seminary were divided administratively into separate entities in 1972. Although continuing to share the same board of trustees and facilities, Virginia College functions as a two-year college while the religious program is conducted under the auspices of the Virginia Seminary. The school's alumni include the poet Anne Spencer and Dr. Noel Taylor, former mayor of Roanoke. Although founded to serve the blacks of central Virginia, Virginia College and Virginia Seminary is open to all and draws students both from Virginia and out of state.

Hayes Hall fell into disrepair in the mid-1970s and was abandoned. Efforts to raise money for its restoration were unsuccessful, and the building was demolished in 1988. Despite the loss of its oldest building and principal landmark, Virginia College and Virginia Seminary remains the Lynchburg area's oldest institution of higher learning and one of the pioneering black-affiliated educational institutions of the South.

118-59

Mid-19th-century print of the Virginia State Capitol

VIRGINIA STATE CAPITOL

Capitol Square, Richmond

Virginia Landmarks Register, November 5, 1968
National Historic Landmark, December 19, 1960

Virginia's state capitol, designed in 1785 by Thomas Jefferson, is one of America's most noted architectural landmarks. Although the capitol historically is identified most closely with the legislative branch of government, several events of special significance to black history took place within its walls. In December 1831 the General Assembly spent much of its session debating the possible abolition of slavery. Impetus for the debate had been supplied by the Nat Turner insurrection. Governor John Floyd hoped that the blood shed by the desperate slaves would move the legislature toward gradual abolition. Contrary to Floyd's wishes, however, the legislature enacted more stringent slave laws and attempted to suppress abolitionist writings. Never again would the South seriously consider abolition.

During the Civil War the Confederate Congress heard a startling message from President Jefferson Davis on November 7, 1864. Manpower shortages had become so acute in the Confederate army that Davis advocated enlisting slaves with the proviso that their service would result in gradual manumission with compensation to their owners. The speech provoked cries of outrage, but ultimately the idea was adopted by General Robert E. Lee. On March 13, 1865, the Confederate Congress passed the enlistment act, but only a few enlistments took place before Lee's surrender less than a month later.

In 1901 a convention of elected delegates met in the capitol to consider a new state constitution. Among its goals was the disfranchisement of blacks. The Underwood Constitution of 1869, many conservatives believed, had been forced on Virginia in order for the state to gain readmittance to the Union. Particularly odious to them were the provisions that enfranchised blacks and poor whites. By the time the convention adjourned in 1902, both groups had effectively been denied the vote.

During the 1950s the General Assembly enacted laws to keep the public institutions of Virginia racially segregated in defiance of U.S. Supreme Court decisions to the contrary. Among the acts passed as part of the strategy of "massive resistance" to the court decisions was one, passed in 1956, that created the Pupil Placement Board. The act divested local school boards and division superintendents of their authority to determine the school to which a child might be assigned and placed that authority with the Pupil Placement Board. Subsequent federal court decisions rendered the board ineffective, but it continued in existence until 1966.

With the defeat of the massive resistance program and the success of the civil rights movement of the 1950s and 1960s in opening public institutions to all citizens, the Virginia State Capitol became more accessible to minorities as well. Many black delegates and senators took their seats in its chambers, including a young Richmond attorney, Lawrence Douglas Wilder. Elected the commonwealth's first black lieutenant governor in 1985, Wilder won the office of governor four years later, the first elected black governor in America since Reconstruction. He was inaugurated on January 13, 1990, with the Virginia State Capitol, once the meeting place of the Confederate Congress, behind him.

127-2

VIRGINIA UNION UNIVERSITY

North Lombardy Street and Brook Road, Richmond

Virginia Landmarks Register, June 16, 1981
National Register of Historic Places, July 26, 1982

The history of Virginia Union University exemplifies the efforts to bring higher education to southern blacks following the Civil War. With the termination of hostilities in 1865, educators faced the challenge of locating teachers and facilities to instruct the many newly freed slaves. Because antebellum laws had prohibited

*Photograph of a typical Virginia Union University student
(J. Livingston Furman) exhibited at the 1939 World's Fair,
New York*

education of any kind for slaves, the vast majority of freedmen were illiterate. Often only the black ministers knew the rudiments of reading and writing. Thus, largely because of the financial support of philanthropic northerners, the ministers launched some of the earliest teaching efforts, directed to educating blacks to become teachers. The Baptist Home Missionary Society formed two schools to serve this endeavor: a Richmond school which later became the Richmond Theological Seminary and the Wayland Seminary in Washington, D.C. Dr. Nathaniel Colver, a Boston abolitionist, headed the Richmond school and was assisted by Dr. Robert Ryland, a local Baptist minister. The Richmond Theological Seminary first was housed in a group of buildings in Shockoe Valley known as Lumpkin's Jail, a complex formerly used as a slave pen.

During this same period interest in the education of black women was growing. Thus in the 1880s a group men and women from Providence, Rhode Island, established a school for young black women in the basement of Richmond's Ebenezer Baptist Church. The school became the Hartshorn Memorial College and soon found a permanent home north of Jackson Ward on North Lombardy Street.

In 1896 it was decided to combine the resources of the Richmond and Washington seminaries. The property of the Wayland Seminary in Washington was sold, and the proceeds were used to purchase land in Richmond adjacent to Hartshorn College. The merger of the two seminaries resulted in the founding of Virginia Union University, a union which was seen as a culmination of efforts to widen the availability of higher education to blacks.

The founding of the university generated the conception of an ambitious building complex. The university commissioned a white architect, James H. Coxhead of Washington, D.C., who designed a series of gray granite structures in the fashionable Romanesque Revival style. The nine buildings in the complex, completed by 1900, constitute an outstanding example of a late nineteenth-century collegiate grouping and stand as a tribute to perseverance and excellence in black higher education.

The new university coordinated its education programs with Hartshorn College, and in 1932 Hartshorn was fully merged into Virginia Union. The university was further enlarged by the incorporation of the Storer College of Harpers Ferry, West Virginia, in 1964. Prominent graduates of Virginia Union University include L. Douglas Wilder, the nation's first elected black governor; and Samuel L. Gravely, Jr., the U.S. Navy's first black admiral.

127-354

MAGGIE L. WALKER HOUSE

110½ East Leigh Street, Richmond

Virginia Landmarks Register, April 15, 1975
National Register of Historic Places, May 15, 1975
National Historic Landmark, May 15, 1975
National Historic Site, November 10, 1978

Maggie Lena Walker (1867–1934), born Maggie Mitchell, daughter of a former slave, rose from modest origins to become a pioneering black businesswoman and civic leader dedicated to improving the fortune of black citizens both in Richmond and elsewhere. Mrs. Walker's place in American history was secured in 1903

Maggie L. Walker working at home

Maggie L. Walker house interior

when she became the nation's first woman to establish and head a bank, the St. Luke Penny Savings Bank.

Maggie Walker's involvement in public service began at age fourteen when she joined the Independent Order of St. Luke, a black benevolent society. She rose quickly through its ranks and eventually headed the organization as executive secretary. Her leadership skills enabled her to increase the floundering society's membership from under one thousand to twenty thousand in a few short years. Among the other posts she held were president of the Council of Colored Women, vice-president of the Negro Organization Society of Virginia, and member of the Executive Board of the National Association for the Advancement of Colored People. She also was prominent in the effort to raise money to found the Virginia Industrial School for Colored Girls, now the Janie Porter Barrett School.

Mrs. Walker established The St. Luke Penny Savings Bank as an outgrowth of her work with the Independent Order of St. Luke. She firmly believed that thrift was a key to success for blacks and felt that a black-owned bank was a necessary vehicle to encourage it. During the period 1903 to 1931, when she was president, the bank became one of the best-managed and fastest-growing financial institutions in the country. In 1929–30 the bank absorbed all other Richmond black-owned banks and became the still-active Consolidated Bank and Trust Company. Her decisive action caused it to be one of the few black banks in the nation to survive the Great Depression. Mrs. Walker served as chairman of the newly organized institution until shortly before her death. In recognition for her many years of service to Richmond's blacks, Mrs. Walker received an honorary degree from Virginia Union University and had a high school named for her.

Maggie Walker's elegant town house on Leigh Street, in the heart of the Jackson Ward Historic District, is maintained as a museum by the National Park Service. Erected in the 1880s, the Italianate dwelling was acquired by Mrs. Walker in 1904 and remained her home until her death. The house has been preserved exactly as she left it, with all her furnishings and other possessions in place. Among Mrs. Walker's many prominent guests in these surroundings were W. E. B. Du Bois, Booker T. Washington, and Mary McLeod Bethune. In 1978 an act of Congress designated the property the Maggie L. Walker National Historic Site.

127-275

Reconstructed slave cabin, Booker T. Washington National Monument

BOOKER T. WASHINGTON NATIONAL MONUMENT

Hardy, Franklin County

Virginia Landmarks Register, January 16, 1973
National Monument Established June 18, 1957

Booker T. Washington was the preeminent Afro-American leader of his generation. To this day his name remains synonymous with enlightened and compassionate racial advancement. With dignity and determination Washington, in the decades following the Civil War, was able to establish widespread respect for the cause of black self-improvement and to become the single most influential American in the areas of race relations and education for Afro-American.

Washington was a living symbol of his goals for the newly emancipated blacks.

Booker T. Washington as a student

He was born a slave on the Burroughs plantation, a low-life establishment in Franklin County, on April 5, 1856. As he stated in his autobiography *Up from Slavery,* "My life had its beginnings in the midst of the most miserable, desolate, and discouraging surroundings." He described the rude slave quarters where he was born as a typical log cabin, about 14 by 16 feet square with no glass windows and a door too small for its opening, where "we slept in and on a bundle of filthy rags laid upon a dirt floor."

With freedom gained following Appomattox, Washington in 1872 at age sixteen enrolled in Hampton Institute where he graduated with honors and later taught. Because of his talents as an educator, he was selected to establish a school in Alabama for blacks that became Tuskegee Institute. The school, founded in 1881 when Washington was only twenty-five, promoted the importance of practical education. Washington was firm in his belief that black students should achieve economic independence through learning specific trade skills, and in the process be instilled with a work ethic and cultural values. Many racial problems, Washington concluded, could be solved once blacks accumulated property and achieved respectability in the eyes of the whites. Tuskegee developed into a model black institution and attracted national attention.

Using Tuskegee as a base, Washington became the country's foremost spokesman for racial concerns. He was an unofficial adviser to presidents McKinley, Theodore Roosevelt, and Taft. President Roosevelt described him as "one of the most useful as well as one of the most distinguished American citizens of any race." Washington realized that full equality for blacks would take many years. He believed blacks had to achieve economic advancement before tackling the problems of segregation and disenfranchisement. His efforts to create better understanding and better opportunities for his people enabled newer generations of blacks to open doors to higher education, political participation, and civil rights. As stated on a monument erected in his honor at Tuskegee, Washington "lifted the veil of ignorance from his people and pointed the way to progress through education and industry."

The Burroughs plantation was conveyed to the Booker T. Washington Birthplace Memorial in 1946. In 1957 the National Park Service acquired the property and has since maintained it as a museum and living historical farm. Washington's humble origins are memorialized with a reconstruction of the slave cabin in which he was born.

33-15

Duke of Gloucester Street, Williamsburg Historic District

WILLIAMSBURG HISTORIC DISTRICT

Williamsburg

Virginia Landmarks Register, September 9, 1969
National Historic Landmark, October 9, 1960

Throughout the colonial period the town of Williamsburg figured strongly in the imagination of slaves as a place of special opportunity. Most slaves in eastern Virginia knew only the drudgery and deprivation of rural life, of endless toil in the fields. Slaves in the colony's capital, however, lived different lives. Many of the urban slaves worked as artisans, including carpenters, joiners, coppers, masons, blacksmiths, shoemakers, cabinetmakers, and coachmakers. Others worked in service occupations such as cooks, butlers, coachmen, gardeners, carters, and barbers.

Town life generally afforded slave men wider opportunities to acquire and prac-

Reconstructed slave living area, Williamsburg

tice a skilled trade than was common in the countryside. However, more slave women and children resided and worked in Williamsburg than did men. "Domestic Negroes," slaves employed in general household tasks, predominated. Tavern and boardinghouse keepers as well as ordinary householders employed slaves, many of them women and children for cooking, cleaning, washing, ironing, tending hearths, baking, sewing, waiting tables, and caring for young children and the sick. Town slaves worked not only for their owners but for other residents who hired their services.

In 1775 half of Williamsburg's population, nearly a thousand people, were slaves. This concentrated population gave town slaves more chances than rural slaves to socialize with other blacks outside working hours. Some slave children also learned to read at the Bray school, an Anglican philanthropic establishment.

Slave work area, Williamsburg

Residence patterns, however, circumscribed the slave's autonomy. Most rural slaves lived with a number of other blacks in dwellings set apart from their owners' houses. In contrast, in the 1780s a third of Williamsburg's slaves lived alone in a white household or else with only one other slave; another quarter dwelt with but two to four other blacks. In town younger slave children usually stayed with their mothers, but their fathers often resided elsewhere in the town or farther away in the country. Many of the hired slaves had to live apart from their families. These slaves slept either in the owner's house or in adjacent outbuildings. Closer quarters in town and fewer slaves per household meant closer supervision of daily life. Some aspects of town life thus may have been more white-dominated than life in rural areas.

In Williamsburg's restored historic district, it is possible to comprehend the urban environment as experienced by blacks as well as whites. Slaves helped to build many of the remaining original buildings. They would have been found working in most of the homes, the shops, the taverns, the college, and the Governor's Palace, as well as at the market and on the streets. The daily life of eighteenth-century Afro-Americans is an increasingly important part of the Colonial Williamsburg Foundation's interpretation of Virginia's colonial capital to many thousands of visitors annually.

137-50

PHOTO CREDITS

All illustrations are from the collections of the Virginia Department of Historic Resources except the following:

Page iv, *Willie Graham, Colonial Williamsburg Foundation; Courtesy of Loudoun County Public Schools; Courtesy of First Calvary Baptist Church*

Page xxii, *Virginia State Library and Archives*

Page 3, *Willie Graham, Colonial Williamsburg Foundation*

Page 4, *Virginia State Library and Archives*

Page 5, *Virginia State Library and Archives*

Page 6, *Virginia State Library and Archives*

Page 13, *Virginia State Library and Archives*

Page 14, *Courtesy of Harvey N. Johnson, Jr.*

Page 18, *Virginia State University*

Page 21, *Collection of the Maryland Historical Society, Baltimore*

Page 23, *Bedford Historical Society*

Page 26, *Courtesy of the Sisters of the Blessed Sacrament, Bensalem, Pa.*

Page 27, *Virginia State Library and Archives*

Page 29, *Virginia State Library and Archives*

Page 31, *Virginia State Library and Archives*

Page 35, *Willie Graham, Colonial Williamsburg Foundation*

Page 36, *Willie Graham, Colonial Williamsburg Foundation*

Page 37, *Willie Graham, Colonial Williamsburg Foundation*

Page 39, *(General John Hartwell Cocke) Virginia State Library and Archives*

Page 40, *Virginia State Library and Archives*

Page 46, *Colonial Williamsburg Foundation*

Page 47, *Colonial Williamsburg Foundation*

Page 51, *Courtesy of First African Baptist Church, Richmond*

Page 52, *Richard Cheek, courtesy of S. Allen Chambers*

Page 56, *Courtesy of Loudoun County Public Schools*

Page 58, *William Edmund Barrett*

Page 59, *Scurlock Studio*

Page 61, *Virginia State Library and Archives*

Page 63, *Press Office, Office of the Governor*

Page 71, *Courtesy of First Calvary Baptist Church*

Page 72, *Courtesy of First Calvary Baptist Church*

Page 73, *Virginia State Library and Archives*

Page 74, *Virginia State Library and Archives*

Page 79, *C. Richard Bierce*

Page 80, *Library of Congress*

Page 81, *Library of Congress*

Page 83, *Courtesy of Fairfax County Heritage Resources Branch*

Page 86, *Hampton University*

Page 87, *Virginia State Library and Archives*

Page 91, *Porter Kier*

Page 92, *Courtesy of Margaret D. Holden, Holley Graded School*

Page 95, *Courtesy of Robert R. Moton Memorial Institute, Inc.*

Page 97, *Willie Graham, Colonial Williamsburg Foundation*

Page 103, *Virginia State Library and Archives*

Page 105, *Virginia State Library and Archives*

Page 111, *Ann Miller*

Page 112, *Courtesy of T. O. Madden, Jr.*

Page 116, *Robert C. Lautman, courtesy of Monticello/ Thomas Jefferson Memorial Foundation*

Page 118, *Courtesy of Monticello/ Thomas Jefferson Memorial Foundation*

Page 119, *Courtesy of Monticello/ Thomas Jefferson Memorial Foundation*

Page 120, *Virginia State Library and Archives*

Page 121, *Virginia Museum of Fine Arts, Richmond. Gift of Colonel and Mrs. Edgar M. Garbisch*

Page 127, *Courtesy of the Newsome House Museum and Cultural Center*

Page 128, *Courtesy of the Newsome House Museum and Cultural Center*

Page 133, *Courtesy of First African Baptist Church, Richmond*

Page 134, *Courtesy of First African Baptist Church, Richmond*

Page 136, *Virginia State Library and Archives*

Page 141, *Virginia State Library and Archives*

Page 145, *Willie Graham, Colonial Williamsburg Foundation*

Page 148, *Courtesy of the Museum in Memory of Virginia E. Randolph, Virginia Randolph Educational Center*

Page 149, *Virginia State Library and Archives*

Page 157, *Courtesy of Richmond National Battlefield Park, National Park Service*

Page 160, *Courtesy of Saint Paul's College*

Page 161, *Virginia State Library and Archives*

Page 162, *Courtesy of Chauncey E. Spencer*

Page 163, *Richard Cheek, courtesy of S. Allen Chambers*

Page 168, *Courtesy of Third Street Bethel A.M.E. Church*

Page 171, *Courtesy of the Hampton Arts Commission*

Page 174, *Planning Department, City of Portsmouth*

Page 177, *Virginia State Library and Archives*

Page 181, *Virginia State Library and Archives*

Page 184, *Virginia State Library and Archives*

Page 186, *Richard Cheek*

Page 187, *Courtesy of the Richmond National Battlefield Park, National Park Service*

Page 188, *Courtesy of the Richmond National Battlefield Park, National Park Service*

Page 190, *Courtesy of the Booker T. Washington National Monument, National Park Service*

Page 191, *Courtesy of the Booker T. Washington National Monument, National Park Service*

Page 193, *Colonial Williamsburg Foundation*

Page 194, *Colonial Williamsburg Foundation*

Page 195, *Colonial Williamsburg Foundation*

INDEX

Virginia Landmarks of Black History: Sites on the Virginia Landmarks Register and the National Register of Historic Places was composed in 10.5/17 Minion; designed, produced, and typeset by Kachergis Book Design, Pittsboro, North Carolina; and printed and bound by Thompson-Shore, Dexter, Michigan.